In Praise of Play

IN PRAISE OF PLAY

Toward a Psychology of Religion

by Robert E. Neale

HARPER & ROW, PUBLISHERS
New York, Evanston, and London

1817

To Rebecca, David, Douglas,
and all children

Contents

Preface ....

Play is a term that has been applied to many of the affairs of nature, man, and God. We speak of a piston rod playing in its cylinder, a fountain playing streams of water, the play of wind on fields of grain, and of the play of otters who fashion slides out of mudbanks and slip on their backs into the water. We see ourselves as players of games and musical instruments, participants in love play, and as players of both ends against the middle. It has even been asserted that existence itself is the play of the gods and that to be in tune with these gods is to be in play. Such frequent and varied usage suggests that almost anyone, anything, or any event can be described as playful.

The purpose of this essay is to offer thoughts in praise of play. The opening chapter presents a psychological theory of play as play, and focuses on the dynamics resulting from two fundamental needs: discharge of energy and design of experience. Work is defined as a result of conflict between these needs, and play is defined as a result of harmony. The theory is amplified by consideration of other theories under the typology of play as work, play as diversion from work, and play as action. Chapter 2 describes play as adventure. The characteristics of adventure are discussed as the elements of peace, freedom, delight, and illusion, and as the modes of story and game. This discussion of play is used to clarify and amplify the psychological theory presented in Chapter 1. In Chapter 3, play is considered from three different points of view to demonstrate that play is not always what it seems to be and that religion may be understood as play. First, it is shown that what appears as play may be only one of the many perversions of play. Then, the possible development of play in the individual is considered with the conclusion that full play in the mature adult is religious. The chapter ends with an analysis of the relation of play and culture.

The remainder of the essay relies heavily on data and conclusions from the study of the history of religions. The purpose of these final chapters is to relate the results of the earlier discussion to an interpretation of religion. In Chapter 4, attention is given to the nature of the sacred and its relation to play. The distinction between sacred and profane is related to the psychological distinction between play and work. Man's ambivalence toward the sacred is diagnosed as his response to the potential for mature play. Three "solutions" to this ambivalence are possible. The religious response is analyzed as that of the player, and the secular and magical responses as those of the worker. The thought is developed in the following chapter by discussion of the nature and function of myth and ritual. Myth is considered in relation to time and story and attention is given to the responses of disbelieving, believing, and make-believing. Ritual is considered in relation to space and sacrifice and attention is given to the responses of suffering without sacrifice, sacrifice with suffering, and sacrifice without suffering. It is suggested that the religious response of the mature player is that of make-believing and sacrificing without suffering. The final chapter recapitulates the themes by considering the central aspiration of religion and gift to the player— death and rebirth. The essay concludes that play is irrelevant and irreverent.

This summary of topic and intent suggests that an essay in praise of play is not an easy venture. It is appropriate at this point to comment briefly on the two limitations most apparent in what follows. The essay is limited in methodology and limited in spirit.

An essay is a composition that deals with a subject from a limited standpoint. There are two clear limitations in methodology in this essay. First, it should be noted that the following discussion is a dialogue with a select number of theories from the disciplines of depth psychology and history of religions. Both the selection and treatment of these contributions are unsystematic. What is chosen is only what might help clarify the nature and function of play. The great number of issues within and between disciplines is ignored.

Second, the theory is incomplete. It is an elaboration of an impression about life that does not aim toward absolute truth. It is noticeably lacking in observations of great numbers of objects. That is, there are not sufficient illustrations of play phenomena to suit the reader who has his own highly individual expectations concerning examples of play. The theory is dynamic rather than descriptive. There is little point in looking at things unless it is known in advance what to look for, and it is a fundamental conviction of the writer that we are blind to the play which is continually occurring in our midst. So, rather than relying on enumeration of a great many observations, the theory is made on the basis of only a few, and by means of what, for lack of a better term, is called "intuition." The theory is also lacking in means for validation. It is a kind of running about in advance of experimentation and documentation. Its value will be determined on the extent to which it fosters new excursions into new realms. The theory *qua theory* is not very important, and the author has no desire that the reader accept it for its own sake. What is significant is play. The only question to consider is the extent to which the theory creates a deeper awareness of the spirit of play.

These limitations in methodology are not so serious as the limitation in spirit. It is difficult for modern man to write and read about play in the appropriate spirit, that is, playfully. Indeed, most would prefer by far to think about work rather than about play. The inescapable bias under which this essay was written and will be read requires preliminary examination.

At the present time, play is thought to be worthwhile for children. Even adults can play if they have not forgotten how and if they do not overdo it. Certainly we must be good sports and play fair. But play is commonly considered as diversion, as not only different from, but also less significant than, other activity. It is suspect because of its power to distract us from the real business of life. To play hooky or be a playboy is to be an idler or a trifler or perhaps even a rebel against society. Society tends to conclude that to play at something while others are working at it is a sign of uninvolvement and irresponsibility. With respect to human beings, it is clear that children may have playmates and adults may participate in love play. But we are not to treat people as toys or playthings. To play with another is considered as an attempt to deceive and curry favor. To play around with members of the same sex can mean making sport of them. To play around with members of the opposite sex can refer to dalliance and promiscuity. The term "play" does have positive connotations such as freedom and pleasure, but it is clear that our society is quite ambivalent about them. Any culture oriented toward work will find play to be incomprehensible and dangerous. A few people will respond favorably to the possibility of play, but many more will respond unfavorably; the vast majority will respond ambivalently.

When play evokes ambivalence, leisure becomes a problem. The current situation of our society is indicated by Robert Havighurst:

> . . . the nineteenth century inner-directed man felt that he should work in order to "make a living." Then, paradoxically, he succeeded in making such a good living that he

produced an economy of abundance in which his grandson
is no longer able to work all his life, but must spend some
of his years in retirement, although he still believes work is
a good thing in itself, and he is suspicious of play.[1]

The questions raised by current reactions to leisure time are
innumerable. Both executives and laborers make far more
money than they need to survive comfortably. Why do these
executives work such long hours, take so few vacations, and
mix much of their leisure with work? Why do the laborers
seek overtime and engage in moonlighting? Why do holidays, Sundays, and vacations fill people with such nervous-
ness? Why do we turn leisure into labor by repairing our
properties and taking grueling automobile trips? Why do
we cut short our free time in order to get back on the job
early? Why does the psychiatric profession speak of "Sunday neurosis" and "vacationitis"? And why, as has been frequently observed, does unemployment lead to suicide and
antisocial behavior?

It is apparent that leisure is threatening to modern man.
It provokes boredom in the individual who does not know
what to do with himself. It elicits shame in the person who
must be important by means of busyness. It gives rise to
guilt in anyone who seeks justification by good works. And
it provokes anxiety in the many whose free time exposes
them to the alienation and meaninglessness of their lives.
So, despite the accusation by some critics that we live in a
"fun" society, leisure is more of a problem than a thing of
promise.

It might appear that this present problem will increase.
In an abundant society which has jettisoned an economy of
scarcity, employment will be postponed and retirement enforced, unemployment will increase, and automation will
replace not only semiskilled and skilled laborers but many
professional people as well. Indeed, there may even be a
guaranteed annual income for all citizens regardless of their

labors. This collision of new abundance with old work ideology has given rise to dire predictions.

But perhaps the threat is not so great as it seems. Those who are concerned about leisure make the realistic assumption that the human being is a "grind" who cannot tolerate destruction of his compulsive routines. If employment by society is no longer required, this ingenious, dedicated animal will escape madness and remain in the everyday misery of work by becoming self-employed. He will be open for business as usual, making himself useful to others and to himself. So, on the one hand, Harvey Cox holds out for full employment "in education, conservation, social work—the areas we call the public sector.' "[2] According to Cox, we should work without financial incentive for the common good. Each individual is to become a benevolent foundation. On the other hand, Robert Lee affirms:

> [Leisure] is a time for rediscovering the meaning and purpose of Life, for seeing the pursuit of living in its wholeness. Leisure is the occasion for the development of broader and deeper perspective and for renewing the body, mind, and spirit. This is the kind of self-learning and self-understanding that forms the basis of true selfhood and provides perspective for the person's involvement in society.[3]

The prospect of being a benevolent foundation or pursuing wholeness for a lifetime is not very exciting, but we can be assured that we will not go mad in a leisure society. Many hopeful praisers of leisure lead us to the conclusion that man is highly flexible and will find more and more subtle assembly lines to maintain his "productive" personality.

The term "leisure" comes from the Latin *licere,* which means "to be permitted." In our contemporary culture, which gives such highly limited permission to be useless, few individuals possess the inner freedom required to respond. Since we cannot permit ourselves to be at leisure but must always be at work or in flight from work, the problem highlighted by current ideological conditions is not leisure but the lack of it. Perhaps what some of the panic-button pushers really fear is the divine madness which transforms everyday misery into adventuresome play. When a work ideology reigns, what we fear most of all is leisure's promise of play. Praise of work does not engender praise of play.

It should be anticipated that the author's vision of play will be veiled by implicit praise of work. Every theory of play under consideration exhibits this bias, and it would be unrealistic to assume that the author is somehow able to escape the presuppositions of his society. The vision of play will be partial and corrupt. But a dim vision is still a vision. Our purpose is to share this vision and discover if contemporaries have seen or can see the same vision. And the question of how one should respond to what is seen or not seen is always secondary. The fundamental task is to discover if the vision can be seen.

Since praise of work is the ruling spirit of contemporary man, this dim vision may well appear as irrelevant and irreverent. The world of play is irrelevant and irreverent—irrelevant to the profane world of the worker and irreverent to the magical god of the worker. This vision of play, like any vision, is something extraordinary, and all intellectual and emotional sets are commonplace by definition. And the reaction of the common to the uncommon is usually "No." But however extraordinary the thesis of the essay, it is nothing new or original with the author. It is found in many creeds and cults in many times and places. There is a minority report throughout the course of history that play is the chief end of man. The ideal attitude of the reader, then, would be a suspension of judgment in order to find out if the vision can be seen. It would be to acknowledge that the vision is irrelevant and irreverent, but also it would be to be possessed by that sacred suspicion that doubts the relevance and reverence of compulsive commonplaces. With this attitude, it may be discovered that the rise and rule of play would make leisure truly a paradise for modern man. Even more than this, it might be concluded that paradise is not only a matter for memory and anticipation as the myths inform us, but also a matter for present discovery. The play which is paradise not only has been and will be on earth, but already is on earth. It is possible to watch for it and be called to participate in it.

ROBERT E. NEALE

In Praise of Play

1 Play as Play ▪▪

EVERYONE has played, but few are able to think playfully about play. It is to be expected that a culture which praises work and considers play problematic will have difficulty in conceptualizing the nature of play. The spirit of the culture prevents the spirit of play from informing the theorists. And it may be that the spirit of play cannot be captured by a theory any more than the wind can be caught by a paper bag.

Consider the following classic episode of play in the life of a small boy. Tom Sawyer has been removed from an anticipated day of play by the verdict of his Aunt Polly. His job is to whitewash a fence of considerable height and length.

> He took up his brush and went tranquilly to work. Ben Rogers hove in sight presently—the very boy, of all boys, whose ridicule he had been dreading. Ben's gait was the hop-skip-and-jump—proof enough that his heart was light and his anticipations high. He was eating an apple, and giving a long, melodious whoop, at intervals, followed by a deep-toned ding-dong-dong, ding-dong-dong, for he was personating a steamboat. As he drew near, he slackened

19

speed, took the middle of the street, leaned far over to starboard and rounded to ponderously and with laborious pomp and circumstance—for he was personating the *Big Missouri,* and considered himself to be drawing nine feet of water. He was boat and captain and engine-bells combined, so he had to imagine himself standing on his own hurri-cane-deck giving the orders and executing them: . . .

"Stop the stabboard! Ting-a-ling-ling! Stop the labboard! Come ahead on the stabboard! Stop her! Let your outside turn over slow! . . . Come—out with your spring-line—what're you about there! Take a turn round that stump with the bight of it! Stand by that stage, now—let her go! Done with the engines, sir! Ting-a-ling-ling! *Sh't! Sh't! Sh't!*" (trying the gaugecocks).

Tom went on whitewashing—paid no attention to the steam-boat. Ben stared a moment and then said:

"Hi-yi! *You're* up a stump, ain't you. . . . You got to work, hey?"[1]

To all appearances, Ben Rogers is playing, and his final re-mark to Tom is most appropriate. But how is this phenom-enon to be defined? Can it be defined in a way that points toward the spirit of play?

This chapter suggests a new theory of play and discusses it in relation to several previous theories of play. The pur-pose is to develop an understanding compatible with the spirit of play. An outline of the dynamics of discharge and design states the theory of play as play. This is followed by analysis of other theories under the rubrics of play as work, diversion, and action. These theories are discussed for three reasons. First, they are presented to give the reader some summary acquaintance with what has been said about play and thus some perspective on the theory of this essay. Sec-ond, they are offered as examples of the extreme difficulty our culture has in thinking about play. And third, they are given as a means of amplifying the theory of this essay. Their inclusion will assist the reader in judging both the nature and value of the theory. The issue is this: Is the play of man really a kind of work in disguise, a diversion from the normalcy of work, so different as to be an act that cannot be defined, or, is the play of man definable as play?

Discharge and Design. One of the most significant theories of play was created by the German poet, dramatist, historian, and philosopher, J. C. Friedrich von Schiller. In the "Letters upon the Aesthetic Education of Man," he stated:

> In the midst of the formidable realm of forces, and of the sacred empire of laws, the aesthetic impulse of form creates a third and a joyous realm, that of play and of the appearance, where she emancipates man from fetters, in all his relations, and from all that is named constraint, whether physical or moral.[2]

Schiller saw man as moved by two basic instincts—the sensuous instinct and the formal instinct—which could function in conflict or in harmony with each other. When the latter occurred, a new instinct of play was created that made man complete and developed simultaneously his twofold nature. Because of this conviction, Schiller could proclaim:

> For, to speak out once for all, man only plays when in the full meaning of the word he is a man, and *he is only completely a man when he plays.*[3]

It is Schiller's basic insight into the nature and possibility of man that informs this essay. To speak of play is to speak of the nature of man. The assertion that we are capable of both working and playing requires a statement about the source of these phenomena. The following theory of play as play is not presented as any kind of final truth, but as a use-

ful way of looking at ourselves in order to understand the
difference between work and play.

The basic premise is that man has a dualistic nature and
is subject both to inner conflict and to resolution of this conflict into inner harmony. The two poles of the duality are
*the need to discharge energy and the need to design experi-
ence.* It is the need to discharge psychic energy that relates
the individual to the concrete and enables him to become
aware of a moment in time and of an object in space. The
need to design and organize experience drives the individual toward the formal and enables him to become aware of
permanency and universality. The former moves the individual to the specific, and the latter moves him to the abstract. Both discharge of energy and design of experience
are necessary for self-awareness. The former provides awareness of oneself as specific and unique, and the latter grants
awareness of oneself as relatively permanent and related to
the natural and human environments. Both full discharge
and full design are required for fulfillment of human potentialities.

These two basic needs are met to some degree in all human behavior. But conflict between discharge and design is
common. It occurs because one of the needs ignores its limits and overrides the other. When the need for discharge
rules, the individual is enslaved by the accidental and knows
only random events. As a consequence, design is destroyed
and inner life is chaos. On the other hand, when the need
for design rules, the individual is enslaved by generaliza-
tions and knows only abstractions. Attachment to the formal
is so rigid that discharge is inhibited and the inner life is
lethargic. Much of human experience can be seen as movement back and forth between satisfaction of the two needs.
The discharge of energy brings the pleasure of contact. But
along with it comes a threat to the design of experience and
the resulting insecurity. The need for design reasserts itself

and regains security, but robs experience of pleasure. Then the need for discharge erupts, and the cycle repeats itself again and again. Since the two needs are in conflict, even the temporary rule by one is limited in satisfaction owing to the equal amount of dissatisfaction caused to the other need.

Conflict between discharge and design is not necessary. Each may accept its limits and excite rather than perturb the other. In this situation, the need for discharge is met and the need for design is empowered; at the same time, the need for design is met and the need for discharge organized. Thus, each need may both assert itself and assist the other. Under these circumstances, the individual becomes aware of himself as both powerful and creative, as both unique and related, and as both changing and permanent. Conflict between discharge and design seems to be inevitable, but it is not necessary. Harmony can and does occur.

A life of continued conflict or of continued harmony leads to general orientations which may be called the *work self* and the *play self*. The individual who consistently is at work in the world is expressing his state of inner conflict. Psychic conflict is intolerable, and resolution must be sought at all costs. From a psychological perspective, *work is the attempt to resolve inner conflict*. The activity of the work self has two characteristics stemming from the battle that inhibits both needs. The first is that the individual is aware of insufficient energy to act. Psychic energy is already engaged in warfare, and there is not enough left over for normal activity. In addition, the individual is aware of a loss of orientation for governing his experience. The deficit is a result of the inner battle. To the extent that some energy and orientation are experienced, they are used to resolve the conflict; that is, they are used for work. All that the individual does is done for the sake of minimizing the battle. He may not be conscious of his inner conflict and only acknowledge an exterior war. So he will work to resolve conflict between himself and others or work to resolve conflict between others. He will appear to himself and others as compassionate and righteous, although his basic motivation is to save himself. The work self created by continual conflict has been deceptive enough to receive great honor among men.

The individual who sees himself consistently as one who is at play in the world is expressing his state of inner harmony. When inner conflict is at a minimum, there is little psychological work to be done. Harmony occurs when the needs for discharge and design both accept their limits and excite each other. Under these conditions, the individual experiences a fullness of power and order. There is neither wildness nor lethargy, chaos nor rigidity, but a coalescence of discharge and design that creates meaningful and graceful movement. Such activity is play. Play is psychologically defined as *any activity not motivated by the need to resolve inner conflict.* Full description of the characteristics of the play self will be given in the following chapters. At this point, it is sufficient to note that harmony does not lead to work in the world. The individual does not need to be an achiever, because he has already arrived. Since he does not have to use the rest of existence for his own sake, he is compassionate and righteous. Of course, workers who tend to equate desperation with dedication normally reject the player as being superficial and uninvolved. The worker's degree of scorn for the player may be an indication of the degree of his own inner conflict. Thus the play self created by continual inner harmony is also deceptive and receives little honor among men.

To conclude this summary statement of the theory, two things should be understood. First, it should be noted that according to the theory outlined, any given activity could be either work or play. The objective nature of an observed activity or what is conventionally regarded as work or play is not being considered at this point. The one thing of importance is the psychological source of the activity; that is, whether conflict or harmony provides the impetus to the action. As will become more clear later, "playing" at the game of golf and "working" at digging a ditch are not always what they seem if one looks beyond the outer conventional appearance into the dynamics of the individual.

Second, it should be understood that states of total conflict and total harmony are theoretical abstractions and not found in a specific individual. Some harmony must be present in the work self or it would not be motivated to continue existence. If conflict is total, there is no desire to survive, and the result is actual death by suicide or psychic death by psychosis. If harmony is total, there is complete absence of concern for survival, and the result is likely to be accidental death. At these two extremes, death is either totally desired or totally ignored. So the conflicted or work self differs only in degree from the harmonious or play self. But this difference in quantity has a qualitative significance which will be described later in detail. At this point, it is sufficient to note that there are two orientations to life stemming from predominance of conflict or harmony, and that these orientations are characterized by the activities of work and play.

What is the relation of our theory of play as play to other theories? All of the theories of play are worthy contributions to the understanding of play. If it appears that the author's critical remarks dismiss them too quickly, it should be understood that this is due to limitations of space and to the illusiveness of play itself. Any theory of play, including that of the author, is limited. If the treatment of the theories seems unnecessarily harsh, it is because emphasis on the problems of examining play is considered to be most important. The focus of concern is play, not any specific theory about play.

Work. The rule of the spirit of work has tended to infect

contemporary theories on the nature of man. The disease is quite apparent in the contributions of Freud and the Freudians. Since they think about play, an examination of their theories will illustrate the common interpretation of play as work. Freud, his creative but orthodox follower, Erik Erikson, and the maverick, academic Freudian, Norman O. Brown, focus on the basic concepts of conflict, mastery, and pleasure. We suggest that these concepts cannot be applied appropriately to play.

The first thing to say about Freud's theory of man in any context is that he begins with clinical observation of psychic conflict. All his theories about man and about play are the product of his endeavor to explain this observation. He concludes that there is inevitable conflict between consciousness and the unconscious, between the basic drives, between the structural parts of the personality, and between the individual and his society. The life of an individual is a history of conflicts and attempts to resolve them. Resolution is never fully attained. Conflict rules, and nearly all behavior illustrates it. There are exceptions to this general statement which can be gleaned from his works, but they are just that—exceptions. Man is portrayed as living in perpetual conflict which ceases only at death.

To state that Freud observed conflict is not quite accurate. What he observed was behavior which led him to postulate the existence of conflict in the individuals he treated. He was led further to suggest that conflict existed not only in those who came to him for therapy, but in all human beings. And he finally concluded that such conflict was an essential part of the human condition and could not be resolved. These postulations could not and cannot be proved in a scientifically rigorous way. Freud himself was led to tell a story or myth of the beginnings of man fully to state his case. But his theory of conflict has been very productive of understanding of man and treatment of man. The theory presented in this essay does not disagree with this postulation of conflict. Freud's genius amounted in part to clarifying what does appear to exist in *most human beings most of the time.*

The issue at stake is whether psychic conflict always has and always will rule to the extent that Freud believed. Are there exceptions to the common state of affairs which he so usefully describes which suggest a revision of theory as to what has been, and more importantly, what can be? We believe that psychic harmony is possible and that conflict need not be pervasive. The issue will probably be decided by the reader in two ways. First, there is the matter of conviction. Freud arrived at one axiom and we arrive at another. The axioms in both cases are a result of intuition and cannot be conclusively proved or disproved. But second, there is the question of usefulness. Which axiom makes human behavior more meaningful? It is our conviction that the behavior labeled as play is made more meaningful by the theory presented. It should be noted that such behavior is considered to be quite rare, an exception to the rule of conflict in human life. On this matter, there is no disagreement with Freud. Yet in science, exceptions do not prove the rule, but demand revision of theory.

Freud's basic understanding of play is derived from the presupposition of conflict. His treatments of the subject are brief, but do illustrate his theory of man.[4] The child at play is considered to be like an imaginative writer, that is, he creates a new world which pleases him more than the world of reality. Play is compensation for required renunciation of pleasure. It can be defined as an attempt to gain pleasure by mastering an unpleasant situation. The presence of conflict leads to the search for mastery and pleasure in play. The latter themes are explored more fully by Erikson and Brown, but it can be affirmed at this point that the most that can be said about Mark Twain's Ben Rogers is that he manifests a somewhat more exuberant *desperation* than that which usually accompanies work. Concrete speculations about Ben from Freud's perspective could be innumerable. His play at being a captain and member of the crew could be an example of the wish to grow up. The possibilities of revenge are obvious. Perhaps Ben has a tyrannical father from whom he escapes and then conquers by becoming a powerful captain. Or, it could be that he is anxious about his bed-wetting and that is why he is a big boat drawing nine feet of water. In any of these speculations, Ben is seen as compensating for the frustrations of his life. He would be portrayed by Freud as a very hard-working boy.

Erik Erikson is one of the most creative among Freud's relatively orthodox followers. His discussion of play expands its definition as an attempt to master. Erikson affirms that the purpose of play is to "hallucinate ego mastery."[5]

This theme is developed by contrasting the play of children with that of adults. After summarizing the adult's freedom in play from gravity, time, fate, bodily drives, and social reality, he points out that such freedom can exist only in a narrow area of life. Erikson equates work and reality, for adult play is that which "permits a periodical stepping out from those forms of defined limitation which are his reality."[6] Thus, adults are essentially workers and can play only rarely. And since they cannot play unless they work, adults are inclined to see the play of children in a false light, as either meaningless or as work. Erikson claims that it is neither. Whereas the adult sidesteps into another reality, the child moves forward to new stages of mastery. The child's play is first centered around its own body; then his play world enlarges to include material toys; finally, his playfulness moves into the sphere of other human beings. Each sphere has its own kind of reality and reflects specific needs for mastery. It is stressed that such play is not the beginning of a drift into fantasy and away from reality, but a working out of adjustment to difficult situations, mastery of new objects, and gaining an identity. It should be noted, however, that Erikson does not completely isolate the play of children from the work of adults. He asserts:

> I propose the theory that the child's play is the infantile form of the human ability to deal with experience by creating model situations and to master reality by experiment and planning. . . .
>
> No thinker can do more and no playing child less. As William Blake puts it: "The child's toys and the old man's reasons are the fruits of the two seasons."[7]

This contribution to the theory of play is valuable as a development of the theme of mastery and of the social aspect of play. But if there is a dynamic difference between the play of children and adults, Erikson has not established it. The child does know some aspects of adult work and steps out of this "reality" to gain freedom. Further, as Erikson himself has shown in a clinical study, the adult may "play" in order to master psychic problems.[8] There seems to be little difference established between the play of children and adults except that the former play more often.

Of course, the basic thing to note is that Erikson defines play as psychological work. Like Freud, he affirms psychic conflict and considers play as a means for overcoming it. According to the dictionary, to master is to overpower, regulate, command, or become adept in. And work is defined as "exertion of strength of faculties for the accomplishment of something . . ." with a stress on purpose, gain, and even compulsion. Common understanding of the two terms suggests that they are quite similar in meaning. Erikson himself sets forth the meaning of work as the production of commodities.[9] Despite his assertion to the contrary, he has defined play as work by his own analysis. The child does not produce a material commodity, but what he does produce, according to Erikson, is *himself as a social commodity*. This commodity is the psychic one of identity that serves the individual only insofar as it equally serves the community. Thus Erikson has related play and work in two ways: (1) Play is the precursor of work and the infantile form of it; and (2) play is really work, in that a desired commodity is created.

Erikson's contribution gives occasion for underlining the distinction between work and the giving of design. The action of the need for design varies under the two selves of conflict and harmony. In conflict, the need creates model situations in order to control reality or to make it appear in accordance with the self's understanding of reality. It functions precisely according to the description given by Erikson, assisting in the task of preservation. However, when the need functions under conditions of harmony with the need for discharge, there is no purpose to be discovered for no need exists which is not fulfilled. It can only be said that design appears for its own sake, or better, for the sake of discharge. Thus the work of mastering and the play of designing experience are two quite different things.

Freud and Erikson approve of play, yet play is praised because it is defined as work. The latter gives this view of Ben Rogers:

> . . . I would see as the "meaning" of Ben's play that it provides his ego a temporary victory over his gangling body and self by making a well-functioning whole out of brain (captain), the nerves and muscles of will (signal system and engine), and the whole bulk of the body (boat). It permits him to be an entity within which he is his own boss, because he obeys himself. At the same time, he chooses his metaphors from the tool world of the young machine age, and anticipates the identity of the machine god of his day: the captain of the *Big Missouri*.[10]

So Ben's play is an attempt to master the body, self, will, and the problem of social identity. It sounds exhausting. If Ben is such an example of a worker, he was not at play and deserves our sympathy. And we who live in a state of inner conflict, who desire to be "productive" personalities, and who cannot permit ourselves to play, deserve sympathy. Like King Sisyphus, we condemn ourselves to the repeated rolling of a huge stone to the top of a hill and do not even allow ourselves the nimbleness of spirit to dance on its revolving surface as it tumbles down. The life we lead calls for sympathy, not praise, when we have lost that nimbleness of spirit.

The eccentric and provocative contribution of Norman O. Brown to the theory of play is a thorough castigation of orthodox Freudian theory and a promotion of the pleasure principle. His earlier book, *Life Against Death*, can be pictured as an extended commentary on two quotations: Freud's uncharacteristically optimistic statement depicts the battle, and the aphorism by Ferenczi describes the adversary.

> Men have brought their powers of subduing the forces of nature to such a pitch that by using them they could now very easily exterminate one another to the last man. . . . And now it may be expected that the other of the two "heavenly forces," eternal Eros, will put forth his strength so as to maintain himself alongside of his equally immortal adversary.[11]

> *Pure intelligence* is thus a product of dying, or at least of becoming mentally insensitive, and is therefore *in principle madness.*[12]

Brown's battle strategy is to use Freud against himself and pure intelligence against itself. The result is a psychoanalysis of psychoanalysis. The goal is to overcome psychic conflict completely.

ianism is based on an understanding that the "reality principle" is a product of the self in conflict. But his alternative
does not seem to be dialectical as he claims but an emphasis
approaching the monistic in favor of the need for discharge.
The two basic needs are similar in nature to the ways of
Apollo and Dionysus to which he alludes. Brown openly
eliminates the way of Apollo as having any positive role in
the psyche. He denies the possibility of a "synthesis" of the
two gods and fails to discuss this denial. It would appear
that he attempts the impossible by cutting the Gordian knot
and hanging on to one of the severed pieces. The results of
Brown's flight are a narrow view of play and a misunderstanding of pleasure.

Since the state of play destroys time, history, and culture
as commonly understood, it is not easy to decipher Brown's
description of the experience. But the proposed rule of the
need for discharge of energy in polymorphous sexuality suggests that the games of marbles, fox-and-geese, and checkers
would not be play but only repressive sublimations. Play,
as commonly observed, has formal aspects which he denies.
It sets up limits in terms of space and time and partakes of
rules and regulations. To add depth and breadth to a common term by means of a new theory is one thing, but it is
quite another completely to distort the term so that it has
no relation to the common meaning at all. At the very least,
Brown's choice of the term "play" is misleading.

Freud, Erikson, and Brown refer to pleasure as a significant element in play, and the latter stresses it to the exclusion of other elements. But pleasure is a manifestation of the
conflicted self. This self experiences both pleasure and pain.
Pleasure occurs, for example, when the demand for discharge of energy gains ascendancy over the demand for design of experience. Yet, since the design demands are being
deprived at the same time, the pleasure is accompanied and
followed by pain. In the state of conflict, pleasure and pain

are inseparable and any victory is also a defeat. Consequently, the work self is always ambivalent, knowing that any possibility of pleasure is also the possibility of pain. It is understandable that such a self experiences anxiety. So the Dionysian exuberance Brown calls for will inhibit the need for design, and the result will be pain and flight from discharge. And if the term "pleasure" be used to describe play, it can be concluded that it must signify a quite different element since play is the product of a harmonious self.

The conclusion is that Brown, despite his superb analysis of the life of conflict and work, still remains within this life. His flight to pleasure may be a sign of a desire for the state of play, but the result will only be more work. Following Brown's analysis, the episode of Ben Rogers indicates, not Dionysian exuberance, but conflict and repressive sublimation. Or, if he would define Ben as playing, our theory suggests that Ben's exuberance is accompanied by pain. In either case, Ben remains in the Freudian perspective as a conflicted self at work. But Brown has attempted to distinguish between work and play. Any such attempt in our culture is commendable. And to equate play with religion is an achievement of high order in any time and place. Brown is responding to a vision which he has seen darkly, but with delight.

The rule of the spirit of work is apparent in these Freudian theories of play. They are valuable approaches to play because they point out the role of conflict and work in most people most of the time, and because they highlight the difficulty of thinking about play. Yet it is concluded that Freudian theory is incapable of describing play because it remains within the limited reality of the conflicted self, and, further, that neither mastery nor pleasure is an attribute of the phenomenon of play. The experience of Ben Rogers and of all human beings who have actually participated in the state of play is not to be analyzed by spoilsports.

Diversion. In a culture that praises work, play is commonly perceived as diversion. Whereas the theorists tend to conceive of play as work, the more informal thinking of the average adult conceives of play as diversion from work. To be diverted is to be turned aside from an important course of action. Thus the play of a bridge game on Saturday night or the play of a Sunday automobile drive is considered to be relatively unimportant. What happens on the weekend may be fun, but it is also frivolous. Consequently, there are people who are ashamed and even guilty over their play. Fun can be frightening to the worker. When play is interpreted as a diversion that detracts from work, time and space for play are liable to disappear.

But play as diversion has also been given a positive evaluation. This very traditional and common-sense attitude is illustrated by a legend of John the Evangelist. It is said that he was once playing with a partridge which he stroked with his hand. A sportsman came along and was astonished to find John enjoying the little creature rather than being busy at work. John spoke: "I see you carry a bow. Why is it that you do not have it strung and ready for use?" The sportsman replied: "That would not do at all. If I kept it strung it would go lax and be good for nothing." "Then," said John, "do not wonder at what I do." It should be observed that play is praised in this legend, not in its own right, but for the sake of work, for the sake of the strung bow which can be put to use. The restfulness of play is restorative. So when play is seen as diversion, the accompanying value judgment depends on whether play is understood as supporting work or detracting from it. In neither case is play judged for its own sake.

There are two theories of play as diversion that suggest the limitations of this view more precisely. Herbert Spencer offered what has come to be identified as the "surplus energy theory" of play.[17] According to Spencer, human nerve centers that are unused are brought to a state of instability and extreme readiness for discharge. The higher animals are more able to provide for themselves than the lower and have time and strength which are not entirely absorbed in fulfillment of immediate needs. The result of this tendency to useless exercise of faculties that have been unused is play. Play is defined as the discharge of surplus energy that occurs when the individual does not have to work.

In criticism of this theory, it has been suggested that animals can play energetically, be obliged to stop from sheer fatigue, and then continue play after only a momentary rest. It would appear that a pair of cats chasing each other will rest only long enough to collect strength rather than be urged on by superfluous vigor. Children and adults may be observed to play long after any such energy would seem to be used up.

This criticism suggests another theory which is the opposite of Spencer's. Instead of seeing play as a way of getting rid of excess energy, it may be defined as a way of recuperating from exhaustion.[18] G. T. W. Patrick suggests that some centers of the brain are overtaxed in modern life and that there is an activity which relieves these centers by involving others not so subject to exhaustion. This activity is called "relaxation" or play. Contemporary life requires a high degree of abstract reasoning, prolonged concentration, and monotonous use of the smallest muscles. The adult plays to recover from the strain of these demands. The child plays because he is not capable of fulfilling the demands of such a society, that is, because he is incapable of working.

This theory has the advantage of explaining why play occurs when an individual is seemingly exhausted. The fact that a student who has read all day can vigorously bowl in the evening is the result of a retreat to a more "primitive" activity. Actually, the theory is only an addition to the one of Spencer. One-sided occupation leaves the other energies

unused, and the playful result is the release of these and
restoration of the lost powers. Thus, the student who bowls
in the evening is both recuperating from mental exhaustion
and getting rid of excess motor impulses. A different illus-
tration, however, reveals that the original dilemma remains.
Suppose that the student does not engage in motor activity,
but turns to his hobby of mathematics and simply substi-
utes for his required reading a treatise on relativity. His
attitude is that of play and he is relieved to have concluded
his study of philosophy, but it can hardly be said that a
physiological change has occurred. The identical brain centers are being "put under severe strain" and the "other centers not so subject to exhaustion" are not involved. The dilemma remains.

The difficulty of these two theories lies in their understanding of play as a one-sided reaction to other one-sided
activity. They view play as a resting of overused powers and
as an exercising of underused powers. But this response to
work is really more work. To play in order to recover from
work is work, and to play in order to return to work is work.
According to our theory, play is not a tool for resolving conflict, but the result of such resolution. It can be concluded
that any attempt to put play in an oppositional relation to
work is liable to end with an implicit equation of play and
work. This danger can be avoided by accounting for the
new energy the theorists observe in a different way. Work
is the result of inner warfare. This conflict consumes a great
deal of energy from the two basic needs. When the conflict
is dissolved, this energy is freed for the harmonious activity
of play. The sudden burst of energy, and of design, is the
result of formerly nonproductive energy and design. So, to
be psychologically exhausted does not mean depletion of
energy, but the presence of much energy and design in conflict. Our theory accounts for the ideas of both excess and
exhaustion, not by claiming play to be a one-sided activity

in reaction to a previous one-sided activity, but by asserting that play involves energy and design in harmony. Consequently, individuals may play even when they seem exhausted, since the "exhaustion" is not true depletion. The exuberance of play is testimony to the vast amount of energy and design that have been at war in the individual.

Whether diversion be judged as an unimportant flight from work, or as an important recreation for work, it is being defined as work. To consider play as diversion is to consider work. So Ben Rogers' personation of a steamboat would be an example of work, either an avoidance of the harsh demands of his schoolmarm, or a preparation for the tasks of reading, writing, and arithmetic when he returns to school. Surely much of apparent play is such diversion. In a work-oriented society, diversion is a common response to more obvious forms of labor. But Ben and some others may not have been entirely caught by this subtle form of business as usual.

Action. If play is neither work nor supposed diversion from work, it might appear to be a phenomenon that cannot be defined. If a work-oriented culture is at all capable of recognizing the spirit of play, it is likely to deem it an unfathomable mystery. Such an approach is an advance over theories of play as work, but not sufficient to please a mind at play with play. Theories of play as action are of this nature.

At the turn of the century, Karl Groos compiled a vast quantity of data, constructed a classification, and offered a biological theory of play.[19] Many of his comments fully reflect the spirit of play, but his basic theory is about play as work. Groos observed that certain important instincts appear in the life of the young animal or child at a time when they are not seriously needed. These are not fully elaborated and are insufficient for any real end. The appearance of these instincts is play, and the purpose of play is practice and preparation for the tasks of survival. Without play, the instincts would perform inadequately and endanger the individual's struggle for existence. Groos concludes, not that children play because they are young and frolicsome, but that they have the period of youth in order to play. Play is an instinct-educator.

This definition of play as practice for maturity has several limitations. It is quite possible that nature is not so carefully calculating as Groos believes. The luxurious and wasteful processes of life suggest that many of the child's actions may be useless for the "natural" goal of preservation. It can be said that any behavior could be useful training for the future, but this would not necessarily be the *intention* of the individual or of nature. Thus, to demonstrate that play often serves a useful function does not prove that play is essentially practice. Further, as Groos himself admits, much of the adult's play seems to be of slight biological significance. These and other difficulties finally lead Groos to a theory of play as sheer action: "In this dilemma we can only hold fast to the fact of the primal need for activity," and he speaks of a universal "impulse to activity."[20] This seems to be no more than a retreat to the common biological truism that activity is a characteristic of life. Indeed, one is tempted to suggest that even members of the vegetable kingdom could be considered as participants in play. And to define play as sheer action is to dissolve the distinction between play and other forms of human activity. Play, and perhaps all varieties of human action, may finally be a mystery, but a definition must create distinctions if it is to be of even provisional use. From this final perspective of Groos, no distinction can be made between the activity of Ben Rogers and Tom Sawyer. So even this commendable nod toward the spirit of play leaves Ben open to capture by the workers of the world.

But the theory of play as action reflects an important aspect of our theory. Play is the way out of a dilemma, an act which cuts the Gordian knot of psychic conflict. Psychic conflict is action, but it is destructive action in that one of the two needs is crippling the other. Work is inhibited action, and at worst, the individual is reduced to the stalemate of inactivity. The action of play is the fulfillment of all action, since the need to discharge energy and the need to design experience are in harmony and stimulate each other. Play is the impulse to act at the highest level, for it is the total involvement of the individual in action.

We began by presenting a theory of play at a fairly high level of abstraction. The theme is that the two fundamental needs of discharge of energy and design of experience function in conflict or in harmony to create the work self or the play self. If this theory is compatible with the spirit of play, then it can be concluded that theories of play as work, diversion, and action are not conducive to understanding play. Specifically, the conclusion is that conflict, mastery, pleasure, rest, and restoration are unrelated to play, and that sheer action does not distinguish between play and work. The many theories of play are reminders of the rule of work and of the difficulty of thinking about play as play. Homo faber is a spoilsport.

After Ben stumbled on him at work whitewashing the fence, Tom Sawyer used all his wit to manipulate Ben into doing the job. Ben was enticed, and, as the author put it, "the late steamer *Big Missouri* worked and sweated in the sun."[21] The author, the readers, and our society conclude that Tom was the victor—"the glorious whitewasher." But if there is such a thing as play, then the actual telling of the story reveals that Tom only got out of work and did not enter into play, while Ben moved out of one adventure and into another one equally exciting. To the player, the conclusion of our society and its theorists is curious.

2 Play as Adventure

OUR UNDERSTANDING of the dynamics of play is so removed from concrete experience that it cannot be used as it stands. If there is a difference between the dynamics of work and the dynamics of play, and between the work self and the play self, then there ought to be distinguishable characteristics in the resulting forms of behavior. Common understanding of work and play suggests that this is the case. The purpose of this chapter is to explore these more concrete differences that have their source in the conflict and harmony of the two basic needs of man.

A term that may convey the spirit of play more than any other is "adventure." According to the dictionary, the noun in the Latin refers to a "happening." The reference is not just to any happening, but to one that occurs by chance, involves risk, and is striking or remarkable in nature. These are three facets of any play activity. From the conscious point of view, play happens by chance—suddenly—as an occasion for surprise and wonder. The adventures of King Arthur's knights, the adventures of Sherlock Holmes, the adventures of hobbits, and the adventures of small boys all reveal the thrill of the unexpected. The factors of risk, hazard, and danger are equally apparent. These are sources of the basic suspense of play where there is no predictable outcome. Whether the contest is with oneself, as in learning to spin a top, with others, as in the game of soccer, or with nature, as in climbing a mountain, results are uncertain and the play is challenging. Even in that mode of play which is largely representational, as in the wearing of a mask or participation in a drama, there is the challenge of an attempt to reveal someone other than oneself and the risk of losing one's own work identity. Also, the phenomenon of play is deemed remarkable by the participant. It is important to note that the player never loses consciousness of the fact that he is playing and always remains aware of the difference between the two worlds. If this were not so, there could be no attitude of adventure, no sense of an unusual and different experience. Thus, to play is to participate in an event that takes place by chance, entails risk, and is of remarkable purport: It is to have an adventure.

Adventure is the result of the player's inner harmony. In the world of conflict there can be no delight in chance, risk, and striking events. The work of the conflicted self is so crucial that events must be made as normal as possible, the strategy must be carefully planned, and the future must be predictable. Spontaneity, surprise, and novelty upset the careful controls of the work self and produce the response of dread. Curiosity and experimentation are limited by reliance on the results of previous work and by fear of failing at something new. The spirit of adventure is quite different. Harmony of the needs provides confidence in one's inner and outer environments. Emboldened by trust, the player overcomes the shock of chance, fear of danger, and suspicion of novelty. Moreover, success is not an issue. As countless observers have pointed out, what is crucial is to play the game and be a "good sport." The kite may become caught in and torn by the branches of a tree; in a formal

phistication. It is the worker who must falsely reduce all
challenges to "manageable" simplicity for the sake of easy
solution. The player is free to enjoy the complications of existence, to be dazzled rather than despairing about them.
Thus, peace is neither inaction nor flight from the human
situation, but a state which produces activity appropriate
to existence—meaningful action.

Second, it should be noted that this peace does not eliminate awareness of conflicts in other people, between other
people, or between oneself and other people. To be at peace
means that inner conflict has been resolved, but not that all
conflict in the world has been vanquished. It is the work
self that can acknowledge *either* inner conflict *or* outer conflict, but not really both. If it acknowledges the former, it
tends to ignore the latter as too much to contemplate, and
vice versa. So there are those workers who dwell on inner
conflict and cannot stand to face conflict in the world and
those workers who dwell on conflict in the world and cannot stand to face conflict in themselves. Understandably,
individuals from these opposed categories clash over priori-
ties of concern, as do certain disciplines which reflect this
distinction, such as psychology and sociology. But the point
is that the worker in either case cannot face conflict fully.
It is only the adventurer who is able to acknowledge genuine conflict in the world. This acknowledgment is inevitable because of the striking difference between his own inner state and the state of the world *and* because the inner
peace cannot be destroyed by outer conflict. To be in the
state of play is not to be threatened by conflict and so to be
able to recognize it fully whenever and wherever it may
occur and engage in it with confidence and enthusiasm.
Thus, inner harmony leads to that state which is characterized by powerful action in the world.

The element of *freedom* is a basic characteristic of adventure which has been duly noted by investigators of play.

What the child experiences can, at the very least, be re-
called by the adult. Consider the varieties of freedom possible and remember what play offered. There may be a sense
of bodily freedom, as in children's gamboling or adult ac-
robatics, where the skip and the somersault defy gravity.
There is an experience of freedom from time, for the small
child who is late to supper because of a game of kick-the-
can lives outside normal time. There is a freedom that tri-
umphs over causality and history, for all players possess
equal chance in a game or equal opportunity to play a role
in a story. There is freedom of the emotions and the intel-
lect, for the player may freely show both positive and negative emotions that do not harm him or his playmates, and
he need have no concern for the creation of useful products
for survival. And there is the sense of freedom from everyday forms of social reality, the players having no work obli-
gations to one another and being free to be themselves, that
is, to be something other than they are in the everyday
world. In summary, the experience of freedom in adventure
is as unlimited as are the forms of human behavior, and the
more comprehensive the play activity, the more complete
the awareness of freedom.

The terms "spontaneity" and "voluntary" are often used in
connection with the experience of freedom. These are both
accurate descriptions of the attitude of the player, but they
do not suffice for a psychological understanding of the phenomenon. The term "spontaneity" emphasizes the idea of an
inner impulse acting without external stimulus, and the
term "voluntary" stresses the concept of choice and consent.
But adventure is influenced by external stimuli, and it is not
necessarily the result of a conscious decision by the player.

A more accurate word for a psychological understanding
of the experience of freedom is "automatic." Adventure is
something that either occurs or does not occur. This is about
all that can be said about it from the conscious point of

view. Many have pointed out that an individual cannot be ordered or commanded to play by another. To be forced to play produces only drudgery. And the opposite is just as true: *An individual cannot force himself to play.* The result can only be a self-imposed drudgery no different in effect from that imposed by exterior authority. It may be that the attempt to have an adventure in obedience to another or oneself may eventually be followed by real play, but the former is not the cause of the latter. Play is independent of either social or private intention. As will be stated more than once in this essay, the author is making no attempt to exhort the reader to "go out and play." An adventure occurs automatically when the needs for discharge of energy and design of experience are in harmony. When harmony exists, adventure is the result. Clearly, this harmony is not the result of conscious decision. The experience of freedom appears when play occurs, but the dynamic point to note is that the player is always *surprised* when an adventure occurs. Thus, the adventurer is a freewheeler in the world who acknowledges his sense of freedom as a gift that can be affirmed or denied to some degree, but never fully controlled.

The new freedom is both freedom *from* and freedom *for*. It is freedom *from* the conflicting demands of the basic needs and freedom *for* new discharge and new design. Such inner freedom does not conflict with the experience symbolized by concepts of causality, determinism, fate, and the like. For in the midst of all the forces that determine and limit the individual, play occurs as a gift which offers a new self and a new state of being. The adventurer is still pushed this way and that by all the forces that push the worker, but his attitude about the matter is quite different. This gift can only be defined paradoxically and metaphorically in thought. The adventurer is one who does not whimper or howl about his fate as the worker does. He does not gripe either crudely or philosophically as is the contemporary fashion. He does not negate existence. The adventurer can dance, even if it is only on that stone which must be repeatedly rolled back up the hill. With a joyous yes to the universe, he freewheels it with fate.

The participant in adventure is a dilettante in the original sense of the term, that is, he is one who takes *delight* in something. A little girl, playing tag around a dining-room table with her father, suddenly stopped to exclaim, "Surely the Lord is in this place!" This is delight. It can be present in varying degrees, which might well be categorized as fun, joy, and rapture. There can be only a quantitative difference between the "put and take" games of the two-year-old child, the love play of two adults, and the primitive's wearing of a mask in a tribal ceremony. This is to say that there is a hierarchy of participation in play that begins in fun and ends in rapture. It is the *amount* of delight that determines this grading on the scale, and the latter has nothing to do with common value judgments. For example, it is possible that a two-year-old may take such delight in a simple finger game that rapture rather than fun is the result, and a pair of lovers may experience fun as well as joy and rapture. Indeed, the amount of participation in delight can fluctuate so rapidly that the lovers will express all three moods during their love play.

Whatever the term used, the observation that play is enjoyable is a truism. But the truism contains several problems of note. Karl Groos, for example, suggests that the player experiences joy in being a cause.[1] This desire to be an efficient cause is regarded as essential to play and deemed the basic source of the "impulse to activity." It is present in sensory and motor activity where it is united with the pleasures of sensation and of activity in itself; it is part of the pleasure of creating imaginative products; and it is clearly present in games of skill and competition. Groos concludes:

. . . joy in being a cause is well-nigh universal since in play
no purpose is served apart from the act itself as impelled
by inner impulse, which thus appears in the character of
an independent cause more than in any other form of activity.[2]

These remarks on pleasure and joy in being a cause require a certain amount of interpretation to be seen as in
accord with our theory. Accepting for the moment the use
of the term "pleasure," it can be agreed that there is pleasure in the inner stimulus as such, in its agreeableness, and
in its intensity. Inner harmony creates the stimuli for discharge and design with new intensity. These stimuli are not
only pleasurable but provide the basis for accepting outer
stimuli as pleasurable, as indicated in the discussion of freedom. But "joy in being a cause" is not a concept fully in
accord with the spirit of this essay. It is the worker so over-
burdened by causality in the inner and outer environments
who desperately seeks to influence these environments. His
struggle for survival demands achievement of power over
events. On occasion he fancies that this has been attained
and takes pleasure in it. But the adventurer is not so concerned. He is aware of himself, neither as being a cause nor
as being beyond causality, but as being a *participant in a
cause*. Groos is correct in observing that "no purpose is
served apart from the act itself." Since the outcome of the
cause is not so significant as it is to the worker, what is of
concern is the participation itself. It is most important fully
to realize that the adventurer takes delight in both success
and failure. If this does not occur, the individual is a worker
who participates in the outcome rather than in the cause
itself.

But the use of the term "pleasure" is ill-advised in a society which labels those who vainly flee work as "pleasure-
seekers." What was mentioned in the previous chapter bears
repetition: the adventurer's delight is quite different from

the pleasure that proceeds from the conflict of the work self. The work self experiences both pleasure and pain. Pleasure occurs, for example, when the demands of discharge gain ascendancy over those of design. Yet, since the need for design is being deprived at the same time, the pleasure is accompanied by pain. In the state of conflict, pleasure and pain are inseparable. Consequently, the conflicted selves of the pleasure-seekers are always ambivalent, knowing that any possibility of pleasure holds also the possibility of pain. Since such ambivalence is intolerable, the work self is eventually led to disgust. The loathing, abhorrence, and nausea that often follow the extreme experiences of pleasure are a result of conflict within a self which cannot tolerate such extreme unbalance. Although delight is quite different from the experience of pleasure-pain, it should not be thought that all negative emotions are excluded from it. There may be danger in the fun, fear in the joy, and awe in the rapture. But as pleasure is undergirded by disgust, the negative feelings in adventure are undergirded by delight. There is delight in the danger, in the fear, and in the awe. It is a commonplace to note that the player even seeks out experiences which challenge his comfort, security, and survival. Thus it is only the attitudes of disgust and delight which are incompatible with each other, the individual being either in basic conflict or in basic harmony.

Delight cannot be described adequately. Insofar as it can be defined as pleasure without pain, a worker can gain some idea of what delight might be like to experience. But the difference between pleasure and delight is qualitative, for the elimination of pain provides such a drastic change that references to the pleasures of man are insufficient. When delight is described positively, the picture must involve hyperbole that rises beyond the limits of logical description. The only way to know about delight is to experience it.

It will be apparent to the reader that the discussions of

peace, freedom, and delight have been more descriptive of the source of these elements than of the elements themselves. This inherent difficulty applies to the discussion of the fourth element of adventure as well. And this difficulty is compounded by contemporary understanding of the term that is used to indicate this element. Play is different and separate from ordinary life. Despite the attempts of some theorists to make it appear so, play is not ordinary. Every adventure contains the element of *illusion*.

The meaning of illusion for modern man is all too clear. We do not care for it. We do not care to play. The scientist speaks of optical illusions, the common man confesses the illusions of his youth and other people's illusions of grandeur, and there are those who call themselves "professional illusionists" because they do tricks for a living. An illusion is a false appearance, something which is erroneous and deceptive. The synonyms for the term are mockery, chimera, and fallacy, while the antonyms are fact, actuality, and reality. The acceptable meaning of illusion amounts to a value judgment on the original meaning of the term. In Latin, the terms *il* and *ludere* are combined to form *illudere*. The former are translated as "in" and "to play." *Illudere* means "to be in play." Illusion is a term which stems from *illudere* and contains the same fundamental meaning. An illusion is something in play, and to be in illusion is to be in play. Now it is perfectly natural to understand play as illusive, and it is even useful to remark upon its deceptive qualities, but the judgment of play as false and contrary to fact and reality calls for some explanation.

The mistake in judgment occurs because the adventurer is discovered by, and exists in, another world and has feelings, thoughts, and behavior that are appropriate to this new experience. In the mildest terms, play is experienced as charming and enchanting, that is, as pleasant and soothing. But these terms have a more traditional meaning that re-

veals the depth of this attitude. The terms "charm" and
"enchantment" bring to mind fairies and elves, witches and
wizards, and they are connected with the occult and the
supernatural. They imply awareness of a new world and the
response of compelling fascination. Both the wearer of the
primitive mask and the player of chess have been bewitched
out of one world by the fascination of another. The reaction
may range from the feeling of pleasantness to the awful
awareness of the uncanny, but at any point along the spec-
trum the feeling is that of experiencing something so different and separate as to be called another world. The source
for this peculiar awareness is harmony of the needs of discharge and design within the individual.

The world man calls his own, however, is the world of
conflict, the world as seen through the eyes of the work self.
No matter how unpleasant it may be, this world is familiar
to him and labeled "reality." The illusion of adventure is
strange for at least four reasons. First, it is a relatively rare
experience for the adult. Its very novelty assists in the im-
putation of deception and falsity. Second, the adult is likely
to find the difference between play and work drastic and
have powerful reactions to it, whereas for most children the
world of "reality" is not so firmly entrenched as it is for
adults. Children move quite freely from one world to another. So the child is likely to find play charming in the superficial sense. Third, the adult may fear not only the battle
within himself but the resolution of this battle as well. Any
inner change may immediately appear to the worker as a
dreadful renewal of open conflict. For those who have gained
some control over conflict by means of suppression and repression, to be caught unawares by play is to be cast into
"fear and trembling." The illusion in adventure is shocking
to those who have lost all awareness of the possibility of
actually resolving psychic conflict. It is, in fact, so shocking
to workers that they have built-in resistance to any real par-

ticipation in adventure. So the new world of illusion is decried as a snare and a delusion.

The fourth reason for this judgment on illusion is the most pertinent. The transformation of a worker into a player and of the work world into the play world is a loss as well as a gain. A play experience can be interpreted negatively because of the possible loss of the work identity and work reality. The experience throws into question the meaning and hope of the everyday world. In this case, the experience of illusion is one of dread and awfulness. Yet the transformation can be interpreted positively because of the gain of a new identity and new world without conflict. The loss is ultimately advantageous. The shock of play remains, but it issues in inspiration rather than in dread. Usually an adult's reaction to adventure will be mixed, both dread and inspiration being present. But the full-fledged worker will be overcome with anxiety alone. He will perceive only the threat of loss of himself and his world. The possibility of a new life in a new world and illusion will remain interpreted as the most fearsome of falsities. The conclusion is that illusion is deceptive for the worker but not for the player.

The judgments of Johan Huizinga and Karl Groos on this subject are worth attention. The former states that there is a representative element in play which is manifest in exhibition and display. A central role is played by the imagination in the making of images. Huizinga allows that this form of play may be only a simple exhibition of something natural, but suggests that it is usually the revelation of something unusual and strange, or, at least, something common shown in a different and bizarre manner.[3] He then affirms that image-making should not be seen as only a sham:

> The child is quite literally "beside himself" with delight, transported beyond himself to such an extent that he almost believes he actually is such and such a thing, without, however, wholly losing consciousness of "ordinary reality."

His representation is not so much a sham-reality as a reali-
zation in appearance: "imagination" in the original sense of
the word.[4]

Huizinga is saying that even though the player participates
fully in an event that is both different and real, awareness
of the common, everyday world remains. Groos' understanding of imagination in play is similar. He also maintains that
even when the player is totally absorbed in illusion, he is
not deceived into mistaking "appearance" for "reality." The
sham activity and pretending objects of play are rarely perfect duplicates of reality, and are, therefore, symbolic. Also,
the feelings of the player toward the most perfect imitation
are never identical to those demonstrated toward the real
object. He argues:

> If such external distinctions alone separated playful illusion
> from actual deception, the force of the former would inev-
> itably decline as this difference increased. But the facts in-
> dicate exactly the contrary, as we may see illustrated by the
> little girl who takes a sofa pillow for a doll; the illusion is
> at least quite as great as when the toy is a triumph of imi-
> tative art.[5]

The conclusion is that make-believe is neither deceptive nor
based on imitation of reality. Groos maintains that a "subtle
consciousness of free, voluntary acceptance of the illusion
stamps even the deepest absorption in it with the seal *ipse
feci* as a safeguard from error."[6] From our perspective, both
Huizinga and Groos are affirming the adventurer's awareness of two realities at the same time. And it can be repeated that unless the player is aware of the reality of the
two different worlds, there is no sense of something different, unusual, and adventuresome. It is the player who is not
deceived by either the world of work or the world of play.

It should be apparent from what has been said that the
adventurer is neither worldly nor otherworldly. Worldliness

is the attribute of the worker who attempts to resolve his inner conflict by a direct attack on himself or by that indirect attack known as "good works." Otherworldliness is the attribute of the worker who attempts to resolve his inner conflict by flight from work. And a flight to sensual pleasure is just as otherworldly as flight to intellectual or so-called "spiritual" matters. The devotees of the flesh and of the cloister are equally on the run from the world of conflict and equally unsuccessful. Adventure is neither work nor diversion from work. Adventure is illusive because it occurs *in this world but is not of this world.* It would be appropriate to speak of play as *un*worldly. The adventurer does not cast out the basic conditions of existence or succumb to them, but is enabled to function according to them in ways which express his full humanity and the full humanity of others. Such unworldliness is better described as new-worldliness. This is the meaning of that illusion of play which is so anathema to the worker that it must be judged as deceptive and false. The conclusion of the adventurer at least is that the element of illusion is the element of reality in play.

Modes of Adventure. The elements of peace, freedom, delight, and illusion occur in the two modes of adventure—story and game. We will consider the nature of these modes with particular attention to the plot of the story and the rules of the game. It will be concluded that, as the four elements are inseparable, so also are the modes. A leading purpose of the discussion is to demonstrate that, contrary to the common opinion that action can only issue out of conflict, full action issues out of harmony, for story and game are both essentially movement.

Playtime is storytime. What Groos refers to as imagination, and Huizinga as representation, issues in the telling of a story. What is a story? A story is news. The latter term has come to be nearly synonymous with knowledge. It is regarded as knowledge of what is going on that might be of interest. This is a pale reflection of an obsolete, but more accurate, meaning. Real news is about something strange. Whether it be good news or bad news, a novelty interrupts ordinary life and a tale is told. The child who smilingly or tearfully tells his mother about an event in school, and the man who tells his wife about a success or failure in business, are not reporting the routine, but communicating the strange. And the verbal telling of a tale is only a sign of that more complete telling which engages the whole interest of the individual. Ultimately, the story is told by a way of life. An adventure is the living of the news, and it is this participation that is the full telling of the tale.

The most important thing to note about a story is that it has a beginning and an end, and that the two are related. This is to say that what is important is the *plot* of a story. The gift of a plot to a human being is what grants him the awareness of *significant identity*. Significance and identity are precisely the result of awareness of beginnings and ends and the relationship between them. The other gift of a plot to the individual is *meaningful movement*. The relationship between a beginning and an end involves action. Plot is movement. To move from a beginning to an end and know the relationship of the two is to be aware of the meaningfulness of the action. So to be an adventurer is to be possessed by a significant identity and meaningful movement.

The source of the story is the harmony of the needs for discharge of energy and design of experience. To understand the dynamics, reference to the plotless life of the worker is useful. The conflicted self experiences the results of the rule of one need or the other, or both in alternation. When the need for discharge of energy rules, the result is chaos. The worker experiences a frenzy of random activity. His identity is not significant nor is his action meaningful, because of the randomness of the discharge. These qualities require the need for design of experience in order to occur.

When the need for design of experience rules, the result is routine. The worker experiences organization of activity in a plodding, rigid manner. His identity is not significant nor his action meaningful, because of the lifelessness of the design. When either discharge or design is lacking full expression, movement or orientation suffers and a plot does not emerge. The typical conflicted self experiences an alternation between the two reigns, participating in a life of compulsive routine occasionally deranged by impulsive chaos. Both the identity and the movement are all the more negative because of the anxiety which occurs in either state. Dread is the symptom of insignificance and meaninglessness.

It is only in play that a story emerges which eliminates both the chaos and routine of the worker. Consider two children telling ghost stories on Halloween. Both have fears of monsters, of the night, and of the unknown. One begins to speak of the awful only to stop with sudden consternation. He meets chaos and then seeks routine. Yet the other child has his fears undergirded with inner harmony and so can complete the storytelling with obvious enjoyment. In harmony rather than in conflict, the two basic needs facilitate expression of each other, so discharge is organized and design is energized. It is only the adventurer who is uninhibited in telling tales. Why else would it be that the participant in a drama is called an "actor"?

There are three elements of the plot of adventure that are worthy of mention—time, outcome, and conflict. Stories for children frequently begin with the phrase, "Once upon a time." The phrase is deceptive, for it is often interpreted as meaning a time in the distant past. More recently, in the realm of science fiction, the stories begin with a more obvious reference to some future time. But storytime is not on the same continuum as the everyday time of the work world. The past and future "times" of the story present the player with a different mode of time. The need for discharge of energy itself knows no time, functions without reminiscence or anticipation, and can be said to live in eternity. Indeed, when this need fully rules over the need for design, the result is a mystical experience of timelessness, whether it occur to the pleasure-seeking hippie or the Oriental mystic. On the other hand, the need for design of experience knows time as chronological, as a passage measured by perception of change, for example, the movement of the heavens and the growth and decay of plants. When this need fully rules, the result is awareness of change. Generally, the two needs are in conflict and time is burdensome; the need for discharge is discontented with the rule of the clock, and the need for design fearful of interruption of its regulation. Eternity is threatened by routine, and time is threatened by dissolution. Work history is duration, occasionally broken up by eternity, but never given significance. Storytime is neither duration nor abolition of time, but the gift of a new kind of time. The appearance of an adventure marks the transformation of duration by eternity, neither remaining as it is but each being transformed into a single awareness of a powerful and meaningful time.

Second, it should be noted that the outcome of a story is not crucial to the adventurer. What is necessary for a story is that it have a beginning and end, not that it have a specific end. This essay has stated repeatedly that success is not an issue for the player. The plot may conclude with "and they lived happily ever after" or with "and the mission was impossible." The adventurer knows that "all's well that ends well" is the wishful thinking of the worker. What is the case is that all is well that simply ends. It is only a story without an ending, which is really no story, that is not well. There is no plot without an end, and with any end, significant identity and meaningful movement occur. What is unacceptable to human beings is not failure per se, but random failure and routine failure. These two kinds of failure are intolerable, while a significant and meaningful failure is more than acceptable. Indeed, it is just as acceptable as significant and meaningful success. What is so disturbing about many modern stories in print and on stage is not that they have negative conclusions to their tales, but no conclusions at all. The difference between *Othello* and *Waiting for Godot* reflects the condition of modern man—the man without a story. Man's actual delight in a tragic story certifies that the nature of the ending is not significant so long as the end truly occurs.

The final point to be noted about the plot of an adventure is that it is filled with conflict. There can be no story without antagonism. No story possesses only a hero. Without the wicked witch or western badman or antagonistic forces of nature, action does not occur. It is necessary to add that such gross examples of hyperbole are likely to occur in adventure but are not necessary. What must be overcome need not always be labeled as evil, but can be something different, or unfinished, for example. The basic point is that this conflict does not reside in the individual, but between the individual and other forces. More subtle still is the fact that this drama can be a psychological one, a story of a psyche overcoming its problems. Even so, the two basic needs of design and discharge are in harmony. It is the interpretation and development of the results of this harmony that supply the conflict for adventure. There is some conflict in the individual in this case, but it is secondary to the basic condition of psychic harmony. This inward adventure is as different from the worker's work on himself as any other form of play.

It is in the understanding of play as story that the elements of peace, freedom, delight, and illusion gain their meaning. If play is always a story that is lived by the player, then it is clear that the peace is an active state of being, that freedom is not opposed to determinism, that delight is other than pleasure, and that illusion is what is most real. Such things occur in man when he is precipitated by the story into another time in which the outcome of the plot is inconsequential and conflict is without his being.

As playtime is for stories, so play space is for games. To play a game is *to be game* for a contest of skill or luck. The game may be largely a game of skill requiring training and discipline, or it may be more a game of chance requiring surrender of the will to fate. Many games involve both factors. In all cases, as Roger Caillois points out, a game creates a condition of equality denied the players in ordinary life.[7] The equal opportunity is provided for the sake of contest. There is something at stake, a victory to insure. This does not necessarily involve a material prize, but may be the honor of being first in power, knowledge, or even luck. Huizinga notes that what is competed for may be simply victory itself.[8] It can be added that the implicit goal is really *to be game*. The prize is the spirit of play.

The mode of game is similar to that of story in many respects, but its special understanding of rules, space, outcome, and conflict requires attention. The question for the reader to keep in mind during the analysis is not only, "When did I last play a game?" but also, "When was I game?"

The most important thing to note about games is that they have rules. As imagination issues in the plot of a story, so it issues in the rules of a game. The rules may be exceedingly complex as in the games of chess and bridge, or they may be very simple and few, as in the game of cops-and-robbers where there may be little more than the rule of dropping to the ground when a bang has been accompanied by a forefinger pointed generally in a child's direction. Usually, there will be rules for the place of the game, for the conduct of the game, and for the beginning and end of the game. The rules of the game serve the same function as the

plot of the story, guaranteeing significant identity and meaningful movement. The rules of the game signify the conditions under which a game can be begun, that is, they point
out the beginning. They delineate the conditions under
which a game is ended, point out the end of the game. And
rules of play proper indicate how to move from the beginning to the end. Thus, like the story, a game has a beginning
and end which are related. And the source is likewise identical—harmony of the two basic needs for discharge and design.

The omnipresence of rules in games leads to the observation that there is no "free play" in the psychological sense.
There are always rules for play, and one who does not accept the rules is not playing the game. Play may appear un-
organized by society, by particular parents, or, as far as can
be observed, by the children themselves. But rules for the
play, although unrecognized by players, will be apparent on
observation and deduction from it. That even the most cas-
ual play of children frequently gives rise to cries of "Un-
fair" and "You're cheating" suggests that rules are implied
despite apparent lack of organization.

The workers are spoilsports with respect to games in two
ways. They may go through the motions of the game without actually accepting the rules. The rules which provide a
game for the player create only a routine for the worker.
In this case, they are a sign of the rule of design over discharge, so enthusiasm is lacking. Or the worker may ignore
the rules altogether. In this case, he is a worker in search of
pleasure as an escape from routine. The need for discharge
turns the rules of the game into annoyances or even threats
to his flight. So the worker is a poor sport who cannot fully
accept the rules of the game. It is only the player who is not
put off but mobilized by the rules.

A second important aspect of games is the use of space.
It would appear that contemporary man is more aware of

time than of space. At least, he complains more about lack
of time than about lack of space. This unawareness may be
a consequence of the absence of space, the lack of an arena
for graceful and meaningful movement. Yet a game requires
a playground which may range anywhere from the small
space of the backgammon board and crossword puzzle to
the fields of football and polo players and even to the entire
life space of the true mature adventurer. Both Huizinga and
Caillois note that play occurs in definite limits of space.
There is a field of play and the sidelines. What passes out of
the boundary is out of play. When a ball or a player goes
out of the play space, the game is stopped for the moment.
The ball is considered "dead," and the spectators are often
considered the same by those who are participating in the
game. What is real is only what is inside the arena.

The role of the basic needs clarifies the nature of this
awareness of the gamester. Awareness of space is perception of objects in relation. The need for discharge of energy
does not know space, only objects. This need ties the individual to the concrete thing. When it rules over the other
need, objects are viewed in isolation from one another. A
single object may capture attention to the exclusion of all
others. Although the superficial mystic may be fascinated
by such an experience, the result is a reduction of the world
into disorder and violence. And the need for design of experience does not know space either, only relations. This
need designs by means of abstractions. When it rules over
the other need, objects are eliminated because they cannot
be organized easily. Probably the most useful and yet most
revealing single abstraction made by man is the concept of
zero, that is, no-thing. Thus, the rule of either need fails
to provide perception of objects in relation, perception of
space.

It is because the need for discharge of energy and the
need for design of experience are in some degree of har-

mony that space is perceived at all. But the two needs are usually more in conflict than not, and space is acknowledged by the worker as burdensome. The need for discharge is unsatisfied with the persistence of relationships, and the need for design is terrified at their possible dissolution by the interruption of things. Since space is always dynamically perceived as that through which one *moves,* it appears as an obstacle course through which the individual moves awkwardly and ploddingly. Space is perceived as run down, and the individual works to sustain it and avoid its destruction. In the end, such awkward plodding becomes paralysis. The worker concludes: "I should have stayed in bed."

The space of the player of games is not the abolition of space, then, but the creation of a new space in which perception of an object is not exclusive and awareness of relation is not abstractive. This space is not heavy or dark, but is light; it is commonly related more to air than to earth. Rather than being immobilized by the weight of space and the fear of spacelessness, the participant is mobilized into full movement. The common analogy is that of flying rather than of walking or crawling. Awkwardness and paralysis are replaced by *graceful movement.* It is this quality of movement which signifies the new world of the adventurer. To play a game is to dance. Full movement is always graceful and awkward action is always inhibited action. An easy way to discover the worker is to look for awkwardness, awkwardness of body, mind, and spirit. To discover the adventurer, the one who plays the game, look for the gift of gracefulness. It can be perceived on the pingpong table and checkerboard, and on any other field of human activity. Play sets boundaries that cut across those set by the work world.

The factors of outcome and conflict require only brief mention because of their obvious role in the play of games. Conflict occurs in games just as it does in stories. Games are competitions and conflict is built into their very nature. Op-

posing forces are required for the game to occur. But, as in
the story, the conflict resides in the game rather than in the
player. Similarly, the ultimate outcome of the game is not
of paramount concern. What a worker finds so difficult to
understand is that a player is fully involved in the game
even so. Better, it is precisely because he is fully involved
that victory is not the ultimate stake. The only thing at stake
is the very game itself—the play of the game. Therefore, the
player is a "good sport." As any sportsman knows, what is
more important than victory is to have played the game. It
is the worker, filled with inner conflict, who cannot tolerate
the outer conflict, and must therefore seek to win at all
costs. He will either quit the game, cheat, or be troubled by
loss of the game. And if he happens to be sufficiently skilled
or lucky to win the game, he will use the event to support
his hope of overcoming inner conflict. Even victors can be
poor sports. It has been observed by most theorists of play
that a game is taken very seriously by the players. It is concluded that such seriousness is a result of the game itself
being at stake. To play a game fully is to be game.

In the understanding of play as game, the elements of
peace, freedom, delight, and illusion also gain their meaning. There is inner peace within the struggling contestant,
the experience of freedom in acceptance of the rules, delight in the battle against other forces, and illusion in the
special space of the new world. Such things occur in an individual when he is precipitated by the game into a new
space in which the outcome of the rules of play is inconsequential and all conflict is outside his psyche.

The conclusion that adventure occurs in the two modes
of story and game should not be interpreted as a perception
of them as antagonistic. They are inseparable, and the division is only for heuristic purposes. There is no story that
is not a game and no game that is not a story. A story creates rules and space, and a game creates plot and time. It

is possible for one mode to be more clearly revealed to the observer than the other, but the less visible one will never be entirely absent.

This conclusion is parallel to that of Huizinga. After asserting that play can be either a "contest *for* something or a representation *of* something," he adds:

> These two functions can unite in such a way that the game "represents" a contest, or else becomes a contest for the best representation of something.[9]

Unfortunately, this assertion is not elaborated upon, for Caillois is of the opposite opinion. Using the concept of game to cover all forms of play, he asserts that not all games have rules, that there are some, such as cops-and-robbers, which involve only free improvisation and are based on the joy of playing a role of make-believe.[10] The feeling of *as if* is considered to replace and perform the identical functions of rules. Further, rules themselves create fictions. So highly structured games such as chess and football may be played "for real," imaginative assumptions being unnecessary. The way of *as if* functions quite differently:

> . . . each time that play consists in imitating life, the player on the one hand lacks knowledge of how to invent and follow rules that do not exist in reality, and on the other hand the game is accompanied by the knowledge that the required behavior is pretense, or simple mimicry.[11]

Caillois concludes that games can either be ruled *or* make-believe, but not both. The above quotations and his own full discussion make it clear that he favors the rules over the make-believe. So Caillois is asserting, in the terms of this essay, that the modes of story and game are incompatible.

Data occur in play which would seem to counter Caillois' view. The common association of wearing the masks and costumes for Halloween and the judging of these in a com-

munity contest is an example of such a fusion of representation and contest. And while rules may not predominate in
the game of cowboys and Indians, there are quite "fixed and
rigid" rules that govern the amount of physical violence al-
lowed, when a player is "dead," how he can return to the
game, etc. To break these rules, even if they be unrecognized until the moment of deviation, is to bring on loud re-
criminations from fellow playmates. So it cannot be affirmed
that play is *either* ruled *or* make-believe.

It has been affirmed that the plot of the story and the
rules of the game serve the same function. Both create a
new world and a new self. It is possible that the plot of a
story emphasizes the new self and that the rules of the game
emphasize the new world, but neither is exclusive. There
can be no new self without a new world and vice versa. The
creation of boundaries and regulations in games will issue in
a new conception of oneself, and the setting of one's personality aside in a story will issue in the formulation of new
boundaries and regulations. The latter is an obvious phenomenon when the make-believe is social, for the play of
two or more individuals together automatically tends to create structure. Certainly there are no fixed and rigid rules
for play with dolls as Caillois correctly affirms, but two little
girls will quickly improvise rules to enhance the game. The
former contradicts Caillois' assertion that competition is a
spectacle only for the spectator and that what he calls "simulation" is absent from the player.[12] It is doubtful that only
the public sees and participates in the drama of a competi-
tive spectacle. In a football contest between a small and a
large college, for example, the drama is that of the underdog
versus the one favored by size, money, and superior training. Certainly spectators will appreciate the drama of the
contest. But the members of the ill-favored team are acutely
aware of their role as well as of the rules of the game. Their
attitude is, "We'll show 'em!" They become, individually, and

as a team, representatives of a contest that is larger than the game of football. Win or lose, they become heroes to themselves, and by this attitude, they may be stimulated to play a better game. Thus, contest may be productive of simulation and simulation may increase and deepen the contest. The two modes of story and game are compatible, inseparable, and finally one in the play of adventure. The significance of this conclusion will become more apparent in a later discussion of story and game as myth and ritual.

The intent in this chapter has been to offer an outline of a dynamic phenomenology of play. The harmony of the needs for discharge of energy and design of experience creates a play adventure in which outer conflict is met by the elements of peace, freedom, delight, and illusion, and the modes of story and game. The final result of this harmony is graceful and meaningful movement.

It is possible now to review the episode of Ben Rogers. He was hopping, skipping, and jumping, munching on an apple, and impersonating a steamboat. If one can set aside the worker's stance of viewing life as just one damned thing after another and the defense of seeking to help others and improve oneself, there is a chance of seeing Ben as a player. He experienced a sense of *peace*. Having no inner conflict, there was no work to be done, no goal to achieve. He was not eating his apple in order to survive, for he had just finished breakfast; but he enjoyed the feel and color of the fruit, the crunch of his teeth on its meat, and the taste on his tongue. Ben took *delight* in his activity. Although the occasion did not call for it, his delight could have included danger, fear, and awe without being destroyed. His "steamboat" could have been an actual raft perilously bobbing in the middle of the Mississippi and Ben would have been just as delighted. And Ben had the *freedom* that is suggested by the child who once defined play as "doing what you want to do and can do." He could not have forced himself to play any more than he could have been forced by others. The drama of the *Big Missouri* was a gift he received and accepted. For a while Ben lived in *illusion*. Living beyond inner conflict for a moment, he had no need to hold on to hard-won defenses, and so gained a new identity and a new world. No wonder Tom Sawyer was envious!

This episode of the *Big Missouri* was both a *story* and a *game*. Although the plot and rules are not entirely apparent, Ben did discover a new time and new space. The harmony created a graceful and meaningful movement. What else could Ben say to Tom but "Hi-yi! *You're* up a stump, ain't you. . . . You got to work, hey?" What Ben knew and Tom did not care to know is that play is the chief end of man.

3 Possibilities of Play ▪▪▪

OUR BASIC theory of play has now been presented. The purpose of this chapter is to form a bridge to analysis of religion as play. A psychological approach to the dynamics and characteristics of play can both narrow and broaden our awareness of its occurrence. Reference to the harmony of the needs for discharge of energy and design of experience and the resulting elements of peace, freedom, delight, and illusion in the modes of story and game suggest an understanding of play that is similar to our common understanding and yet somewhat different. Much of what is commonly known as play does not necessarily fit the definition at all, and some of what is not commonly associated with play may be exemplary. This chapter will aim at deepening understanding of play possibilities in three ways. First, it will consider the negative possibilities of perversions of play, those activities that appear to be play but are really work. Second, it will examine possibilities in the maturational development of the individual, those activities that appear to be work but are really play. Finally, it will outline more general possibilities with regard to the relation of play and culture.

Perversions. The observations made thus far have reflected only the *ideal* manifestation of play in human behavior. A more realistic appraisal is required. First, it can be briefly noted that conflict and the work of overcoming it is the existential norm. The value of Freud's basic understanding of the human condition cannot be overestimated. Play occurs rarely and briefly. The conflicted self is only occasionally and most momentarily replaced by the harmonious self. Thus, the adventures of man are few and far between. A full life of adventure is exceedingly uncommon, and even such a life probably will be more ruled by the work self than by the play self.

Second, discussion of the characteristics of play assumed, for the most part, the presence of *complete* harmony of the two needs. In such an ideal case, play is the inevitable outcome. Yet, in fact, the harmony is nearly always partial. Conflict and harmony are not fixed states and the relationship between them should be represented as a continuum. Man lives between the two extremes with a degree of both. Either may be in ascendancy, but neither may totally rule. Therefore, although there is opportunity for the response of play to partial harmony, there is also opportunity for the response of work. Adventures may not occur, and the spirit of work may rule instead. The result is neither harmony alone nor merely conflict, but a mingling of both. The newly released energy and impetus to design from the partial harmony is acknowledged, but it is used for the sake of achievement in the world of work. The conflicted self is not destroyed, but remains to use the new energy and order for its own purposes. The result is neither play nor obvious work, but perversion of play.

It is common understanding that the activities of the poor sport, the cheat, and the playboy are not really play. The poor sport who complains about the imbalance of teams or accepts his defeat ungraciously lacks the elements of play. The cheat who breaks the rules has neither the spirit of adventure nor respect for games, but seeks to win at all costs for the sake of overcoming psychological conflict. Nor is the playboy, despite his title, a participant in the world of play. He may be more subtle than the poor sport or cheat, but his dalliance with women and yachts is compulsive, a neurotic attempt to deal with basic conflict. At best, the playboy is *trying* to play, and the result is disguised work. He is a drudge. Pleasure may occur, but delight is entirely absent. And probably boredom is more his lot than the momentary excitations of pleasure. So it is clear that not all who participate in commonly accepted forms of play are really players. All such disguises of work that ape play are a result of the mingling of harmony and conflict within the individual. Harmony presents the possibility for play, but conflict presents the occasion for perversion of play. The nature of these perversions can be seen more systematically as perversions of the four elements of play, perversions of the two modes of play, and perversions that arise from the attempt to preserve play.

Because the elements of peace, freedom, delight, and illusion must all be present in play, suspicion of perversion should arise when one or more appear to be absent. But even when all four appear, things may not be as they seem. There are four perversions, each aping one of the basic elements of play.

It has been noted previously that the peace of play is peaceful action. The perversion of this attitude is the "peace" of *in*action. When conflict between the needs is acute and evenly balanced, the result is a stalemate. Shock leads to immobility. Psychological peace is not identical to stupor. Or the momentary but rigid control by the need for design may appear as peaceful. In this case there is not the peace of harmony, but only an apparent calm before the storm of open conflict. There may be some action, but it is a suppressive or repressive action that disguises conflict rather than witnesses to its defeat. Calm pastimes may be involuntary masks for that raging conflict which immobilizes the individual and allows only minor distractions. The game of solitaire can be no more than an automatism, like a facial tic, that indicates the need for discharge and design.

The perversion that apes freedom occurs as a result of the momentary ascension of one of the two needs. The impulsive individual feels free from control, and the rigid personality feels free from chaos. Yet there is an awareness that the other need will soon rise from the underground and replace the one that rules. This freedom is a freedom without hope. Further, there is an awareness that this freedom is really bondage, that one really becomes a slave of the dominant need. The perversion of the element of freedom is entirely negative, being a freedom from one need and a bondage to the other. Thus, the father who takes time and space to "play" catch with his son and yet worries about whether he should be doing some paperwork for his boss, is not really playing. Such "play" is, at best, a symptom of the uneasy freedom of man in rebellion from conflict and will not be accompanied by the elements of peace, delight, and illusion. Only the positive freedom that actually incites both needs to fuller activity will be associated with all the other elements of play. Where this freedom is lacking, real play becomes a perversion of play.

The perversion of delight is what is usually termed "pleasure." Its source and distinction from delight have been fully noted previously and need not be repeated. Just recall the faces of those attending a cocktail party. Common visages of grim satisfaction render the message, "I'm having fun no matter how much it hurts me." It can be emphasized, however, that this may be the most deceptive of the perversions of the elements of play. The perversions of peace, freedom, and illusion can be noted as such fairly easily by those who are so inclined. But the worker commonly defines his pleasure as play. He and his society believe that he is having fun in his flight from work. This perversion is pervasive and society is persuaded that play occurs.

The element of illusion is not limited to the world of play. It is a pervading characteristic of obsessive-compulsive neurosis and of many forms of psychosis. Mental illness is generally understood as a highly limited, but nevertheless, real attempt to solve a problem. Such illnesses are products of the world of conflict, being work reactions to work problems. The feeling of the uncanny is the result of the "return of the repressed." However, this "return" requires repression of the other need, whereas in play the ruling need is not deposed. In both cases, the element of illusion occurs, but in the mentally ill the reaction is one of dread and terror due to the loss of control and destruction of personality, whereas the player is benefited by the gain of a new order and a new self. The different dynamics insure that the mentally ill will not experience the feeling of illusion in conjunction with the other elements of play, but the player will experience peace, freedom, and delight as well. Of course, it is not necessary to be mentally ill in order to experience this perversion. A mild-mannered girl who discovers her aggressive tendencies while playing a role in a high school drama may find her spirit of play shattered rather quickly. The perversion occurs whenever one responds negatively to a revelation about a new self or new world. Such revelations are common and usually rejected.

When one or more of the perversions of the elements of play exist, the spirit of adventure does not occur. Usually the imitations of play will be of brief duration and followed by more open manifestation of conflict. At worst, the individual will be cast into *boredom* and experience that languid weariness of action and listless discontent with life which truly reveal the absence of play. Simply filling up time and space by attempts at play is commonly and cor-

rectly perceived as "killing time and space." That many contemporary commentators on our society find boredom to be
a pervasive aspect of contemporary life suggests that adventure is very rare.

The fundamental perversions which occur in the modes
of story and game are those of the four elements of play.
But discussion of the modes gives occasion to comment on
a perversion of story, a perversion of game, and a perversion
that both share in common.

Caillois states that a corruption of story, that is, what he
refers to as "simulation," takes place when "the one who is
disguised believes that his role, travesty, or mask is real."[1]
The key concept related to this perversion is that of belief.
The nature of belief will be considered extensively in later
chapters, but it is useful to note at this point that belief is
an attribute of work, and to be permanently and completely
caught in a foreign role is a result of a compulsive attempt
to flee the world of work by means of a work mechanism.
Pity the person who cannot take his mask off when the play
is over. He was never at play. Such belief is a workmanlike
response to illusion which destroys it by making it a commonplace "truth" or everyday "reality." Play has limits, and
when these are abandoned, the results are the impersona-
tions of the mentally ill.

Sometimes the worker is somewhat aware of his perversion. Probably because of a bias against the element of simulation, Caillois does not comment on the distinction between *pretending* and *pretension*. The latter is the perversion of play-pretending. When a group of children all tell
marvelous stories to illustrate how superior their fathers are,
the spirit is one of pretending. But when the group is asked
to give mundane information about their fathers and one
child persists in relating the marvelous, pretension may be
ruling in his reply. Pretension occurs in one who is at least
somewhat aware of what he is doing, that is, aware of the

fact that he is using a mask to deceive another without his consent. This is quite distinguishable from the deceptions of the professional magician or even the dramatic actor which are presented before a knowing and willing audience. The pretender uses his disguise for gain in the struggle for existence in the world of conflict. Pretension is a sign of need rather than of fulfillment. Every worker runs the risk of becoming a confidence man.

The corruption of game is most commonly related to its rules. As has been previously stated, the worker breaks the rules in law or in spirit by cheating, establishing his own rules without consent or even knowledge of the opponent, or just attempts to submit his enemy to a ruthless beating without breaking a rule. Any victory is liable to be vindictive, and defeat will be followed by despair. Thus, for a game to be interesting to a worker, it must be "played" at the expense of others. Many apparent players are inhibited from corruption by other needs, but even the rise of a temptation to cheat indicates existence of a work mentality. And in games of solitaire, the inhibitions are frequently overcome.

The final perversion relates to both story and game. It has been repeatedly affirmed that an adventure is not a sure-fire success. An adventure is a happening which involves risk. A story may end in tragedy and a game may be lost. Play is always a gamble, and if the gamble is removed or even the attempt to remove it occurs, the play is perverted. Now the attitude of our society toward gambling is quite ambivalent. Specific games of chance and those who haunt them have a bad name, but those who speculate on the stock market are considered, unless they engage in unethical practices, aboveboard. There are many reasons for this, such as the association of criminals with the former type of gambling, and also the attraction of such games to the terrible compulsions and cravings of very disturbed people. Compulsive gamblers are workers, but it is clear that stock market speculators can be workers also. From the psychological point of view, the chances are that the majority of gamblers, regardless of the specific game they are attracted to, are workers trying to deal with their conflicted selves.

The question to ask is whether the gambler, whatever his game, focuses on the winnings or on the game itself. For example, the average professional gambler with cards or horse racing does work for a living and focuses on the winnings. But there are exceptions, such as the recent but fabled "Nick the Greek" who gambled for large sums of money, being a millionaire one day and penniless the next. The money itself was put to little use, much of it being given away to hatcheck girls or simply mislaid. He did not willfully throw it away but was unconcerned about it. "Nick the Greek" was a professional whose activity, at least in this particular realm, suggests more the spirit of play than that of work. Again, most amateurs may gamble for the enjoyment of wagering rather than winning. But there are many who gamble in order to improve their everyday existence, if not in terms of financial success, then in terms of prestige. The obvious games of chance may or may not be occasions for play and what is determinative is the dynamics of the individual.

There are really two signs of perversion of the risk of adventure in story and game. One sign is the attempt to influence the outcome by tinkering with the element of risk. As Caillois observes, this leads frequently to superstition and magic.[2] Lucky pieces and much of the little rituals that have grown up around popular games demonstrate a magical attempt to beat chance. Many gambling systems are little more than such rituals. It should be noted that this insight eliminates much of the child's activity which is frequently magical in nature, especially that which depends on belief in the omnipotence of words. And it is rare to find a team in any game which does not develop a set of customs to help its success in the sport. The other sign of this perversion of risk is fatalism. When the element of chance is too much for the worker in attempted play, he unhappily concludes that he has no control over events. Such acknowledgment of chance by despair considerably contrasts with the player's delight in risk. The conclusion is that neither magical optimism nor pessimistic fatalism is appropriate to the state of adventure. An adventure both begins and ends with the unexpected. Without full acceptance of the unexpected, all stories and games are perverted.

The final group of perversions of play are the most tragic of all, for they are attempts to uphold the fragile and delicate spirit of play and preserve the adventure. The perversion occurs in three ways, two relating to the reaction of the player's society, and the third to the player's own experience of play.

When the phenomenon of play is received indifferently or hostilely by a work society, the player may be tempted to respond with either secrecy or promotion. Play is always *display,* a public phenomenon basically opposed to secrecy. Participation in the guessing game of "I've Got a Secret" can be playful only if it is assumed that the secret will be disclosed. If the holder of the secret does not intend to reveal it, the game is work. And there is a difference between a secret and a mystery. A secret is defined as something explainable but concealed from understanding, whereas a mystery is something that cannot be explained. The player takes delight in the mystery of play for its own sake. The desires of the two needs being fully satisfied, he has no need to hide mystery by beclouding it with secrets. Consequently, the one who *uses* mystery by attempting to transform it into a secret is not a player but a worker. The worker cannot tolerate mystery, so this transformation is protective of the work self and has the additional advantage of creating outsiders who are not in the know. And whoever proclaims, "You can't play with me!" is not playing. Further, those whom the revelation of secrets entices to join esoteric "players" are liable to be *disillusioned* by the discovery that no mystery is present. Thus, secrecy destroys rather than preserves play.

The other reaction, that of promoting play, is equally destructive. The attempt to change the attitude of the opponents of play, to win them over and invite them to become players, is inevitably a defensive manifestation of work. What is communicated to others is work rather than play, and those who are persuaded are often led only to a work imitation of play. The true player does not attempt to change others, although he freely accepts those who care to join in his play. This does not mean that he is silent or inactive in the presence of others. An invitation is extended but not belabored. To offer a gift is one thing; to sell a commodity is quite another. The player witnesses to his enjoyment because he can do no other in the abundance of the play spirit. It is this spirit itself which is contagious. As the blossoming plant does not need to be potted to bring the bees to the nectar, so play does not require additional enhancements. And, as the pot may kill the plant, so promotion may destroy play. It is by having an adventure rather than by defending and promoting it that its spirit is communicated.

It can be noted that somewhat allied to the perversion of promotion is the curious practice that is called "play therapy." Along with the promoters of play, the child psychotherapists often assert that play assists in the solution of personality problems. To the contrary, the understanding being developed by this essay is that play does not solve anything, for it is the *result* of resolution of psychic conflict. One can only claim that when the problems of work are solved, play will be the result. Therefore, play cannot be promoted as beneficial to mental health or anything else. It can only be said that the individual who does have an adventure is a healthy and fortunate person. Accordingly, what is termed "play therapy" would be better entitled "work therapy," which means that it is not really play at all. And, even though the reader wearies of it, it can be added that this essay is not an attempt to promote play in the sense mentioned above.

The final perversion of preservation has nothing to do with society's reaction to the player, but is a consequence of the individual's own attitude. And it is this perversion that is the most difficult for the worker to understand. Adventures do come to an end. Stories and games are not interminable. And a story or game is not necessarily followed by another one immediately. Anyone who has experienced what seems to be play may be tempted either to make it last or to force a return of the apparent play state. But play cannot be promoted by and for oneself any more than by and for someone else. Obviously, work cannot produce or sustain play. Play itself can be, and often is, highly repetitive, but such repetition is the result of harmony rather than of conflict of the two needs. When a compulsion to continue or repeat play experience occurs, the result of such going through the motions is legalism and scrupulosity. The effort to control play not only fails but actually creates more work. Its best results are dutiful observance and wistful remembrance rather than participation in high adventure.

It can be stated that whenever the "player" finds it difficult to stop "playing" and regrets the end of "play," real play has not occurred. The facts of psychic life are that harmony is not always in the ascendancy and that play is continually concluded and replaced by conflict and the necessity of psychic work. It is the player and only the player who can accept this fact. The worker cannot accept it. The individual who cannot stop "playing" is actually a worker who has taken pleasure in his diversion. This momentary pleasure is due to the victory of one of the needs, and the individual is avoiding the conflict that has not been resolved. He does not want to let go of the pleasure for fear of the pain that will inevitably follow in increased measure. He does not care to pay for his flight from conflict as he must. The real player is absolutely free to stop playing whenever the play is finished. He who experiences delight rather than pleasure has received all, and even more than, he expected. As the poet Heine proclaimed, "Once I lived like the gods, and more is not necessary." Because of this attitude, the player freely returns to the self and world of work. He does not face the powerful retribution that the worker does, but returns to work on far more equal terms with the basic needs. Imbalance exists, but it is not so great as that occurring in the worker who has gained only pleasure. The reaction of the player to the end of play is *gratitude* for all that he has received. He returns to everyday life with the thankfulness that grants courage and hope in the world of work. This gratitude, then, enables him to accept the conflict he must face. It is the attitude of gratitude and the attitude of grimness that distinguish the player and the worker with respect to past enjoyment. This perversion of preservation truly separates the worker from the player. The former is like the little boy who responded to a call to supper, "Aw Ma, I'm not hungry. . . . Can't I play some more?" More rare is the playful response, "Gee Ma, am I hungry! . . . and did I have fun!"

The perversions of adventure have been analyzed as perversions of the four elements of play, perversions of the two modes of play, and perversions that arise from the attempt to preserve play. Owing to the near omnipotence of the world of conflict, the occurrence of only partial harmony, and the fragility of the play world, these perversions are overwhelmingly common. So the first thing to say about the possibilities of play is that they are exceedingly limited.

Development. If play is not always what it seems to be according to common understanding, then there are likely to be activities that appear to be work but are really play. Just as a small boy may be "playing" cops and robbers in order to solve his personal problems, so may an adult approach his "job" in the spirit of play. For example, a lawyer may find that the process of writing a legal brief grants him the peace, freedom, delight, and illusion of play. He may be so engaged in the game that he does not worry as he ordinarily does about the consequences of his action, "working" longer and harder at the brief than the possible amount of financial reward justifies, and "working" with little regard for whether or not he will win a favorable decision. In this situation, the lawyer is earning a living, but this is a fortunate by-product of his basic state of play. The adventures of man may be few and far between, but they do occur and may well be unrecognized. An adventure is always a surprise, and the time, place, and form of the adventure will be surprising. So the possibilities are not only less than is commonly supposed, but also greater than usually acknowledged. The idea to be presented now is that *maturation of the individual presents the opportunity of growing from playlessness to full play and that full play in the adult is religion.*

In the beginning, there is no play. Knowledge of psychological dynamics during the first year of life is limited and highly speculative. Whether the finger and facial movements occurring during the early months of life are actually the result of harmonious relation between the needs for discharge of energy and design of experience is impossible to determine. But it seems probable that the newborn infant operates only on the basis of pleasure and pain. He is either satisfied with sufficient food, dry, and well-fondled, and so participates in the bliss of sleep, or he is extremely unsatisfied and responds with cries of suffering and rage. The latter response is assurance enough that the narcissistic life of the infant is not the paradise some psychological utopianists have made it out to be. It is likely that the human being is born with problems to be solved. But from the time of toddlerhood on to the very moment of death in old age, the spirit of play can be observed.

Maturation of the individual allows an increase in the breadth of play. The infant, if indeed he does play, is limited to activity with his body and the nipple of the breast that feeds him. As the child develops, play may come to involve other objects, feelings, and thoughts. Although it begins as a private activity, it may become "parallel" play, and then group play with social rules. It can be noted that the early ways of play are not necessarily left behind, for the adult can return to the simple forms of a child's play or he can incorporate them in his more advanced play. Children's play is contagious, and there are undoubtedly some mothers whose enjoyment of peekaboo is not entirely a consequence of pleasing the child. The adult game of charades certainly incorporates the five-year-old's delight in facial gestures and imitations into the more intellectual realm.

It is useful to speak of *partial play* and *full play*. Full play for the infant may be physical only. The adolescent whose play is only physical is only partially playing, for the other possibilities offered by maturation are absent. So playful participation in a game of football is closer to full play than the stunt of juggling three oranges if the individual has reached the juvenile stage of development. A twelve-year-old boy playing chess is not so close to full play as the one who builds an artistic snowman in competition with others.

Full play is that which uses all the potentials offered at the particular developmental stage of the individual's physical, psychological, and social growth.

Most discussions of play development end with the stage of adolescence and the addition of a few remarks to the effect that the adult also plays. The implicit suggestion is that the adult does not play very much, that his play is relatively unimportant, and that when he does play, the activity is similar to that of the child. But the adolescent discovers new realms of human activity—the areas of sex, vocation, and philosophy of life. These new possibilities are commonly seen as matters of work only, but they present possibilities for play as well. There is no category of adult behavior that cannot be play as well as work. Whatever can be experienced as conflict between the need for discharge and the need for design can be experienced as the resolution of conflict. The adult who limits his play to such activities as golf and amateur theatricals is unfortunate, and the theoretical limiting of adult play to such activities is obscurantism. What is commonly understood as adult play is only partial play. Full adult play, a mature adventure, would encompass all the fundamental concerns of the mature human being, including those of sex, vocation, and philosophy of life. Only when the total personality of the adult is involved can the activity be seen as full play. Needless to say, the total personality can also be involved in full work. It is only when harmony of the psychic needs is in ascendancy that the possibility of full play occurs.

Three things about this idea of maturation into the possibility of full play should be noted. First, an objective criterion has been added to the definition of play. Up to this point, it has been repeatedly stressed that nearly any human activity could be a manifestation of play. The only criterion presented for determining the kind of behavior was the presence of psychic harmony. But the final judgment on the play of an individual includes the range of his play as well as simply the appearance of play. This more objective criterion has just as important a role in the understanding of play as the other one. We believe that some play is better than no play at all. An individual whose only area of real play involves the solving of crossword puzzles is more fortunate than one who experiences only psychic work. But such vast realms of the possibilities of play are unrealized that he hardly represents an ideal manifestation of adventure. Although his mind is engaged in play, it is quite possible that his body and emotions are not. And, most importantly, the potentialities of play with other human beings are not fulfilled. The human animal is a social animal. Play that does not involve other human beings probably does not involve the individual's concerns in sex, vocation, and philosophy of life. Further, it can be said that the more narrow the individual's range of play, the more suspect it is. For play is contagious, not only in the way it is caught by other people from the player, but also in the way it catches on in the individual. It has the tendency to spread from one area to many others. The spirit of play naturally expands to incorporate more and more of the total personality. Pleasure, on the other hand, does not have this movement, but tends to remain isolated in the presumably safe areas of life. So, the more narrow the play, the more the individual's play is partial and the more it is likely to be work.

The second point is that the player, at least the full player, is social. He is frequently accused of lacking concern for other people. Actually, it is the worker, despite his serious proclamations to the contrary, who is unconcerned. He dashes here and there in the world and keeps very busy doing good deeds for his neighbors. But the problems he perceives and works upon in the world are projections of his inner problems. He is concerned about himself, and the ambivalent response to his belligerent doing of good works only dumfounds him. The player has no inner conflict and, therefore, no need to be concerned about himself. He is free to respond to other people for their sakes and not his own. He does not abuse his fellow men by using them as the worker necessarily does. He simply recognizes their existence. He is always surprised by them. And he is surprised most of all by the fact that they are working themselves to death. So the player does suffer, but *he suffers because others work, not because he works.* That is, he suffers for others rather than for himself. Now the player does not busily rush in to pick up the pieces of their fragmented lives. Rather, as a jester or clown, as a messenger from the realm of comedy, he demonstrates another way of life by his own behavior. The player lives as an example of what could be in the lives of his neighbors. His play is contagious, and some get a glimpse of a new world and are enticed into adventure. His suffering remains as long as there are workers in existence. But this suffering does not diminish his delight, for he remains in play, embarked on an adventure with these workers. So the true and full player is highly social and yet totally irrelevant to the world of work. An adventurer among men leaves the world of work behind and indicates the way to another.

The final point moves to the basic theme of the essay. Full play by the mature adult can be understood as the end goal of human development. Obviously such an experience is quite rare. The adult remains on the work level for the most part and his entries into the world of play are partial, relating only to certain aspects of his life. But the ultimate experience does occur, and when it does, although it is similar to all the partial adventures that have preceded it, it is of such greater breadth as to seem entirely different. And the experience is labeled as it has always been labeled—it is called "holy." Like Moses before the burning bush, the mature player takes off his shoes and kneels on holy ground. And like David before the Ark of God, he also kicks up his heels with delight.

Play and Culture. Consideration of the perversions and maturational possibilities of play suggests that it does not always occur according to cultural stereotypes. Play is forever surprising. Some theorists have been sufficiently surprised to relate play boldly to culture and religion. The remainder of this chapter begins discussion of these two possibilities of play. The theories of Schiller, Huizinga, and Caillois have not been selected as the most representative of those pertaining to the complex relations of culture and religion, but as illustrative of the place of play in this realm of interaction. The purpose of the discussion is to provide perspective so that association of play and religion will not appear meaningless or blasphemous to modern man. The essential conclusions can be stated briefly. On play and culture, it is concluded that both play and work are basic sources of culture. On play and religion, the preliminary conclusions are as follows: the sacred is the realm of new discharge and new design; religion is the playful response to this new world; magic is the work response to it; and the profane is the world of work.

Schiller's praise of play amounts to a praise of the aesthetic.[3] He finds his solution to the problems of culture in the harmony of what he calls the instincts of sensuousness and form. Natural physical man is selfish, violent, and destructive of society. Society forces him into political fetters which rob him of his freedom and actually prevent the rise of true morality. The problems of individuals and societies are solved by the harmony of the instincts which issues in the spirit of play and fosters the beauty of living form. Moral law and all other areas of value for man have no autonomy, but are grounded in the aesthetic disposition, cre-

ated and sustained by the instinct of play. It is the realm of
aesthetics in which play fully appears and in which all other
areas of life find their meaning.

Schiller's approach raises the question: Is play more than
an aesthetic phenomenon? The difficulty of the theory is
that it begins with the harmony of the two instincts, continues with the appearance of beauty, and then ends with
the creation of true morality. The particular progression is
nowhere fully justified. It could be claimed just as easily
that true morality is the source of beauty. But neither bias
is supportable. "Living form" in man's response to nature
is beauty, and in his response to human nature, it is morality. To degrade or eliminate either response is to pervert or
forfeit a relation to part of existence. The conclusion is that
the harmony of the two instincts of sensuousness and form
creates both beauty and morality on the same level, that
both are equally products of the harmony and of equal status in the hierarchy of creation. Consequently, no quarrel
between them is possible, and the individual must participate fully in both nature and human nature.

Schiller's fundamental insight that the harmony of the
instincts, or in the terms of this essay, needs for discharge
and design, issues in the instinct of play remains valid.
What is eliminated is the common and unexamined opinion
that the phenomenon of play is more inherently a part of
art than of other responses to life. The Western understanding of aesthetics is to be given credit for appreciating the
play element in art and for preserving an understanding of
play as related to mature human behavior, but lack of appreciation of play's existence in morality and religion has
tempted it to overextend its claims. That moralists and re-
ligionists have also lacked this appreciation of play and supported the bias suggests only that it will be difficult to overcome.

The subtitle of Huizinga's *Homo Ludens* is "A Study of

the Play Element in Culture." He finds that play is present in law, for justice is commonly decided by contest; in war, for fighting is regulated by honorable obedience to rules; in philosophy, for the latter is an intellectual duel involving riddles and disputations; in poetry, for verse is literally a playing with words; in music, dance, and the fine arts, for all these involve contest and representation; in customs as well, such as in the constantly changing forms of human apparel; and, most importantly, play is present in the rituals and myths of religion. In all these realms, Huizinga documents his thesis that play is ever-present in culture. The narrow association of play and aesthetics is abandoned for a more comprehensive understanding of the pervasiveness of play. Moreover, play is considered to be not only an element in culture but its primary source. Huizinga writes:

> The view we take in the following pages is that culture arises in the form of play, that it is played from the very beginning. . . . It is through this playing that society expresses its interpretation of life and the world. By this we do not mean that play turns into culture, rather that in its earliest phases culture has the play-character, that it proceeds in the shape and mood of play. In the twin union of play and culture, play is primary.[4]

Huizinga has no static conception of the relations of play and culture. Although play is the source of culture and the shape of the first manifestations of culture, it slowly passes into the background. Play is primarily absorbed into religion and the remainder into philosophy, the arts, folklore, and the various forms of social life. Eventually the play element becomes totally disguised. Huizinga considers Western history to illustrate this theme. From the time of the classical Greeks to the last century, the element of play was clearly manifest. Huizinga demonstrates its presence in Roman culture, in medieval life, and in the Renaissance, Baroque, Rococo, and Romantic ages of Western culture. But the last century illustrates the decline of play in culture. "All Europe donned the boiler-suit," and utilitarianism and technology came into the forefront of society. Although it might seem that the predominance of sports and increased leisure activities signifies a heightening of play in the present century, Huizinga claims that the systematization and regimentation of modern man enters into his leisure time and destroys the true element of play. In business, art, and science, the element is also severely curtailed. Modern social life is little more than false play. Yet Huizinga believes that possibilities for appearance of play remain. Play is so connected with culture that it cannot be completely severed from it. It may return in the warfare which throws the individual and the masses into the intoxication of an immense game. Or it may return in the more benign form of the fulfillment of civilization. Such a return is required for the continuance of true culture. It is as necessary now as it was in the very beginning.

The contribution of Huizinga is valuable because it takes the element of play out of captivity to the realm of aesthetics by demonstrating its role in many of the major areas of human activity. But, like any theory of play, that of Huizinga's is open to criticism. A more systematic comparison of play and nonplay in culture would have been ultimately more elucidating and preserving of the fragile play spirit. The breadth of his praise of play is not matched by depth.

His basic proposition that play is the source of culture and most present in early manifestations of culture is certainly debatable. The more familiar anthropologists become with primitive peoples, the less able one is to romanticize about them. Their work activity appears less exotic and more recognizable as work. And some of their apparent play has been revealed to be of significance to them as work. It cannot be concluded that play once ruled absolutely. And the decline of play in contemporary man may not be so great as Huizinga proclaims. It is possible to play while wearing a boiler-suit and to play with technology. The systematization of leisure time need not destroy the spirit of play. Thus, Huizinga's historical analysis might have had more depth if some understanding of psychological dynamics had been included.

A fundamental objection to Huizinga's positing of play as *the* source of culture is made by Caillois in his discussion of play as basically independent of ordinary life.[5] What he considers to be the fundamental elements of play—competition, chance, simulation, and vertigo—are equally present in ordinary life as well as in play. In ordinary life they are out of balance, excluding each other and destructive of life, whereas in play, they are neither unbalanced nor dangerous. Because these realms of play and ordinary life are entirely separate and equally fundamental to man, Caillois concludes:

> In the end, the question of knowing which preceded the other, play or the serious, is a vain one. To explain games as derived from laws, customs, and liturgies, or in reverse to explain jurisprudence, liturgy, and the rules for strategy, syllogisms, or aesthetics as a derivation of play, are complementary, equally fruitful operations provided they are not regarded as mutually exclusive.[6]

Caillois' view that Huizinga has oversimplified and overextended the application of play to culture appears correct. Following our theory, it can be affirmed that the relations of the needs for discharge and design issue in work and play and that these two fundamental types of behavior are equally sources of culture.

In this brief setting of perspective on the role of play and culture, it has been seen that play can be an element in many aspects of life other than the aesthetic, and that both play and work are involved in the creation and maintenance of culture. The contributions of Schiller and Huizinga are reminders that praise of play is not always playful in spirit. Both praise play as the source of what man regards most highly in civilization. They are inclined to ignore the role of play in what man does not regard so highly. But play does not limit itself to areas of great human concern. To praise it for its role in art, law, and other dignified areas is likely to be praise for the usefulness of play. This is the praise of a worker. By contrast, the player keeps his eye on the sparrow.

As an aspect of culture, religion can be related to play. Both Huizinga and Caillois raise issues pertinent to the theory of this essay. Huizinga affirms a primal relationship between play and religious ritual and myth. He demonstrates that ritual contains all the elements of play. Ritual is considered to be pre-eminently "a matter of shows, representations, dramatic performances, imaginative actualizations, of a vicarious nature."[7] The attitude of the ritualist, like that of the player, is deemed to be one of joy and make-believe. Myth is understood as having similar characteristics. Above all, it is noted that myth is so filled with absurdities and enormities that it must be accompanied by a considerable amount of humor. Huizinga concludes that religious myth and ritual are the prominent areas for the appearance of the spirit of play.

However well Huizinga has caught the spirit of play in religion, his treatment of the issue raises important questions concerning both the relation of the sacred and profane and the relation of religion and magic, as these fundamental divisions of life relate to play. The problem of the sacred and the profane is illustrated by comparing the doll play of a little girl with the fondling of a small idol by a primitive man. According to Huizinga, both the child and the adult are playing. Such a postulation is hardly acceptable to the religious sensibilities of an adult. No criterion is given for the distinction between adult religion and the seemingly profane play of the child. What is required in addition to Huizinga's analysis is understanding of the difference between partial and full play. When the play spirit rules the total personality, the result is mature religion, and when the play spirit rules only part of the individual, the result is partial play regardless of whether the individual is a child or not. The play of the child and the religion of the adult remain intimately related, as the difference is only *quantitative*. When religion is acknowledged as full play, it follows that the full play of the child is religious also, even though immaturely so from adult perspectives.

Huizinga's presentation is also unsatisfying because it does not deal conclusively with the nonplay element in man's response to the sacred. The great difficulty with his thesis concerns the response of magic to the sacred. He observes:

> According to ancient Chinese lore the purpose of music and the dance is to keep the world in its right course and to force Nature into benevolence towards man. The year's prosperity will depend on the right performance of sacred contests at the seasonal feasts. If these gatherings do not take place the crops will not ripen.[8]

Now, to be "seized" by an event and to help an event come to pass are quite different things. The attempt to manipulate and control nature and the divine is hardly a manifestation of play. Huizinga criticizes Frobenius for stressing the manipulation and de-emphasizing the playfulness of such manipulation, and then does nothing but reverse the order of importance and ignore the problem. It seems sensible to conclude that the nonplay element has become mixed with that of play, that the sacred and the profane are no longer separate. For magic is the perversion of full play, a "making use" of the new energy bestowed by the sacred for the purposes of the profane realm of work. Since such profane intrusion is common in what is called "religion," no such simple equation of play and religion as given by Huizinga is sufficient.

The basic approach and final conclusions of Caillois on play and religion are quite different from those of Huizinga and raise the problem of magic more fully. In his article, "Play and the Sacred,"[9] Caillois praises Huizinga's contribution and agrees that play and religion have much in common. But, after adding material to support Huizinga's thesis, he then argues that the attitude of the player and that of the religious person are completely opposed. Since play removes man from "reality," the player is not any more involved in an activity than he chooses to be in advance. This is the source of freedom and security. Also, the consequences of the activity are severely limited, for one can always stop playing. The player is the master of his destiny. So the good player does not complain about bad luck or losing in a competition because the content and results of play are not crucial to his being. In sum:

> . . . one is led to define play as a free activity in which man finds himself immune to any apprehension regarding his acts. He defines its impact. He establishes its conditions and conclusion. From this derives his ease, calm, and good humor, which are not merely natural but even obligatory. It is a point of honor with him not to show that he takes the game too seriously, even in the event of ruin or defeat.[10]

The above remarks on the attitude of the player demonstrate that play is quite different from ordinary life and, Caillois affirms, from the sacred as well. Whereas content is not important in play, it is thought to be highly significant in the sacred. The content of the sacred is "an indivisible, equivocal, fugitive, and efficacious force."[11] On man's relation to this force, Caillois writes:

> Rites serve to capture, domesticate, and guide it, for better or worse. Compared to it, man's efforts remain precarious

and uncertain, since by definition it is superhuman. He would be unable, in any case, to control it at his pleasure and confine its power to limits fixed in advance. Also, he must revive it, tremble in its presence, and supplicate it in humility.[12]

Consequently, play may be seen as a relaxation and forgetting of life, whereas the sacred creates tension and new dangers. Moreover, the sacred is separated from ordinary life, not because the sacred is fragile as play is, but because the sacred is a dangerous force which might destroy ordinary life. Finally, it is affirmed that whereas play is an escape from ordinary life and ineffective in the transformation of this life, the sacred is responded to precisely in order to transform real life and insure success in the gambles and competitions.

Caillois believes that the individual feels as rested and refreshed when moving from the sacred to ordinary life as when he moves from ordinary life to the realm of play, and that in both movements there is an awareness of a new degree of freedom. But play is only a diversion from real life, whereas the latter is only a diversion from the sacred. Caillois concludes with the following theory:

> Therefore, a *sacred-profane-play* hierarchy needs to be established in order to balance Huizinga's analysis. The sacred and play resemble each other to the degree that they are both opposed to the practical life, but they occupy symmetrical situations with regard to it. Play must dread it. It breaks or dissipates play at the first collision. Conversely, one believes that it depends upon the sovereign power of the sacred.[13]

Two comments are pertinent to this argument between Caillois and Huizinga. First, the former's assertion that the player is in complete control of his activity is rarely, if ever, true. Huizinga is more correct in his assertion that there is

an uncertainty and risk in play. The child does not necessarily intend to be frightened by the sound of his voice imitating the roar of a lion. The adult may lose his life by
motorcar racing or mountain climbing. The attitude of adventure includes caprice as well as control. In the world
of work, risk is forced onto and feared by the individual,
whereas in play, risk is freely accepted and even freely
sought. The player does not choose his destiny as Caillois
claims, but follows a destiny which is revealed to him during the course of his adventure. It is for this reason that
play is feared by the worker who is truly the one who seeks
mastery of destiny, and it is for this reason that the player
does not complain of bad luck. Caillois is right to claim that
play is of no consequence in the ordinary world, but he has
no basis on which to claim that it is of little or no consequence to the individual as player. This distinction between
play and religion does not stand.

Caillois is quite right in claiming that Huizinga does not
fully account for the attempt to capture, domesticate, and
guide the "force" which is fundamental to the sacred. Yet
he equally ignores Huizinga's illustrations of the joyful
make-believe which is so clearly a part of primitive religion.
To reconcile these two points of view, it can be said that
there are two ways of responding to this primary force. The
force is the result of the unleashing of energy which was
formerly contained by inner conflict. If there is acceptance
of this new energy, the result is play. If the new energy is
feared, the result is perversion of play, a semiretreat to the
world of work in an attempt firmly to control and use the
new energy for goals of the work world. Consequently, the
play reaction to which Huizinga refers may be called religion, while the work reaction to which Caillois refers may
be called magic. The sacred is power and the responses to
it may be either religious or magical. Huizinga and Caillois
each have dealt with only one side of man's reaction to the

sacred. It is the conclusion of this author that a new hierarchy is required to replace both the theory of the identity of play and religion proposed by Huizinga and the hierarchy of *"sacred-profane-play"* proposed by Caillois. The new hierarchy is that of *sacred-religion-magic-profane*. This conclusion is fourfold: (1) the sacred is the realm of new discharge and new design; (2) religion is the appropriately playful response to the sacred; (3) magic is the inappropriate work response to the sacred; and (4) the profane is the world of work. By means of this conclusion, some of the fundamental insights of Schiller, Huizinga, and Caillois are retained and a means of resolving their differences made possible.

Thus far, we have considered the dynamics, characteristics, and possibilities of play. It has been concluded that man has the basic needs to discharge energy and design experience which may be in relative conflict or relative harmony. The work self is the creation of one who must use most of his time and space to attempt resolution of inner conflict, whereas the play self is the creation of one who experiences that coalescence of discharge and design which leads to the significant identity and meaningful and graceful movement of adventure. Play is distinguished from work by those elements of peace, freedom, delight, and illusion that occur in the modes of story and game. And much of what appears to be play may be a perversion of play, while some of what is not commonly associated with play may be exemplary. It is possible for adventure to capture totally the life of the mature adult, and this full play is the experience of the holy. The sacred is the realm of new harmony of discharge and design, and religion is the play response to it. To this possibility of religion as play we will now turn.

4 Play and Religion ....

It is difficult, if not impossible, to indicate the nature of religion very precisely. Its seemingly universal characteristics are neither so universal nor so characteristic as frequently thought. Neither the existence of gods or spirits, belief in the afterlife and cosmology, practice of prayer and sacrifice, concern for the ethical, nor the existence of a specialized priesthood is absolutely required. Many definitions of religion are contradictory. Some have said that religion is what a person does with his solitude. Others have said that it is what binds men together. Psychologists have defined religion as having its source in fear, or in sex, or in the emotions in general, or in a "religious instinct." Perhaps the most important of all definitions, although rarely stated openly, is the one given by Parson Thwackum in Henry Fielding's *Tom Jones:* "When I mention religion, I mean the Christian religion; and not only the Christian religion, but the Protestant religion, and not only the Protestant religion, but the Church of England."[1] It may be impossible for any human being to escape the spell of this type of definition.

The issue is complicated by the presence of magic which, although somewhat ignored by students of contemporary religion, is undoubtedly as rampant now as it ever was. Discussion of magic and how it differs from religion is equally difficult. It has been said that magic is private, whereas religion is social, but this distinction may not do justice to Christian hermits and mystics who lead a solitary religious life. It has been affirmed that magic is impersonal whereas religion deals with a personal god, but this distinction reduces much of Buddhism and mysticism in general to magic. Again, it is common to state that magic is manipulative and religion petitionary, yet it is easy to claim that a petitionary approach to the divine may be no more than sophisticated manipulation. Perhaps the most important of all distinctions, although rarely admitted openly, is the belief that magic is what the other individual, village, or nation believes in. Or magic is what I *used* to believe in, or what we all *used* to believe in. The common definition is: Magic is that which I do not practice. It may also be impossible for any human being to escape the spell of this type of definition.

In acknowledgment of these difficulties in considering religion and magic, there will be no attempt to offer a final definition of them. Our purpose is only to suggest an understanding that may add to other discussions a dynamic view of the role of work and play in relation to the holy. This is to say that this chapter is parallel to the first chapter of the essay. Its conclusions on the dynamics of work and play will be used in conjunction with the theories of Otto, Van der Leeuw, Eliade, and Caillois to arrive at a dynamic understanding of religion. And it is necessary to begin, not with religion per se, but with what religion is a response to—the sacred. Thus, there are three areas of concern to be considered: first, the distinction between the sacred and the profane; second, man's ambivalence toward the sacred; and third, the three possible "solutions" to this ambivalence which are the secular response, the magical response, and the religious response. Consideration of these three issues will provide an introduction to the dynamics of religion as play which will be given more concrete examination in the following chapter.

Sacred and Profane. It seems sufficiently obvious that to have an experience of the holy is to have an experience of something different from what is usually experienced. If this were not the case, the experience could not be labeled as holy. The having of an experience implies that some *difference* has occurred. Despite the logical and experiential necessity of this understanding, there is a tendency among some modern students of religion to blur, abolish, or simply ignore any distinction between the holy and the secular. But the historians of religion under consideration not only distinguish between, but assert that the sacred is the *opposite* of, the profane. So what is, in everyday understanding, a truism requires some explanation and confirmation.

In *The Idea of the Holy*, Rudolf Otto refers to the object of religion as the "Wholly Other":

> . . . that which is quite beyond the sphere of the usual, the intelligible, and the familiar, which therefore falls quite outside the limits of the "canny," and is contrasted with it, filling the mind with blank wonder and astonishment.[2]

The mystery of the "Wholly Other" is not a problem that can be solved; it is unsolvable and "incommensurable" with man's faculties. Otto observes that the extreme statement of this separation of sacred and profane comes from the mystics who speak of the object as "nothing" or "void." Such speech contrasts the "numinous" with all that is known by negation, and yet retains the positive quality of that which is completely foreign. At least, this is the intention of the mystic himself. Those who have not had this experience are unaware of the need for caution in description of it, and are prone to dismiss the "no-thing" or "no-common-thing" quality of the experience as simply "nothing." On this topic, as on so many others, the one who has had the experience frequently speaks less and more guardedly than the one who lacks the experience. Otto concludes that the distinction between sacred and profane is absolute.

Van der Leeuw begins his book, *Religion in Essence and Manifestation,* with the affirmation that the first thing to be said about the object is that it is the "Other," that it is totally different from all that is commonplace and familiar.[3] The initial state of mind of the primitive man is *amazement* at what is completely unusual. This dumfounding quality of all religious experience suggests to Van der Leeuw, as it should to all who study it, that the sacred and profane are totally separate.

Mircea Eliade asserts that "the first possible definition of the *sacred* is that it is the *opposite of the profane.*"[4] The sacred is known because it shows itself as something different from the profane. Eliade demonstrates how the homogeneous space of the profane is broken into by the sacred in the creation of a sacred space that founds the world by providing orientation, and how the ordinary temporal duration of profane time is broken into by the sacred in the creation of sacred time, that is, by a return to the mythical time of beginnings. The objects of nature, the tools of man, the functions of eating, sex and work, or any other elements of human experience, may be the occasion for the manifestation of the sacred. This is to say that the sacred can manifest itself in nearly any place, time, and through any medium. The sacred does not occur in a vacuum but in the midst of the profane and common. But it should not be concluded that the sacred-profane dichotomy is annulled by the manifestation of the sacred (which we may call a hierophany) in any mundane object. Every such hierophany is paradoxical. Eliade argues:

> What matters is that a hierophany implies a choice, a clear-
> cut separation of this thing which manifests the sacred from

everything else around it. There is always something *else,* even when it is some whole sphere that becomes sacred—the sky, for instance, or a certain familiar landscape, or the "fatherland." The thing that becomes sacred is still separated in regard to itself, for it only becomes a hierophany at the moment of stopping to be a mere profane something, at the moment of acquiring a new "dimension" of sacredness.[5]

Thus, although the hierophany is considered to be paradoxical in that any object can remain itself and yet become something else as well, Eliade maintains a clear distinction between, and separation of, the sacred and profane.

This paradox is present in religion from the most primitive to the most sophisticated beliefs. The sacred stone of the primitive is both fully a common stone and fully the uncommon sacred, and Jesus the Christ is both fully a common man and fully the uncommon God. What becomes so difficult to understand in the complicated communications of theologians is a matter of common experience which every human being has had. Certain times, places, objects, and persons take on a special significance which does not destroy but adds something different to the commonness. This experience reaches its peak when the paradox is of the sacred and profane. They remain distinct and separate.

Roger Caillois agrees with the above authorities, but sharpens the paradox by emphasizing that the sacred and profane are "mutually exclusive and contradictory."[6] On the one hand, the sacred can destroy the profane, for the profane man who accidentally touches a sacred person or object may die. On the other hand, the sacred may be altered and weakened by the profane, so sacred places and persons are protected from unworthy individuals. Thus, the antagonism between the two requires protection for both. During ordinary life, the sacred is experienced usually as taboo and defined as "the guarded" or "the separate." This means that when the profane rules, the sacred is seen as negative and destructive of the profane. But at the time of a festival, the dull continuity of quiet labor is abolished by the explosion of the sacred into communal life, and all work for survival becomes taboo. Moreover, the festival is frequently characterized as a time of violence and promiscuity; all the common mores become taboo. Thus, when the sacred rules, the profane is seen as negative and destructive. The two are not only distinct and opposite, but incompatible.

Caillois adds to the mysterious nature of this experience when he suggests:

> . . . they are both necessary for the evolution of life—one, as the environment within which life unfolds; the other, as the inexhaustible source that creates, sustains, and renews it.[7]

The conclusion is that the sacred and profane are both antagonistic and complementary. Consequently, there are *consecration* rites for the sake of the sacred and *deconsecration* rites for the sake of the profane. As another example, it can be noted that primitive society is frequently bifurcated into groups that are both antithetical and complementary, what is sacred for one group being profane for the other. So Caillois concludes that the sacred and profane are not only distinct and opposite, but also antagonistic and complementary.

The conclusions of these authorities combine to form the first and most important thing to say about the sacred—that it is different from the profane. A psychological understanding of the sacred and profane will be slowly developed throughout the following discussion. At this point, it is necessary only to draw attention to the fact that play and work are also distinct, antagonistic, and complementary.

Part of the burden of the first half of this essay was to distinguish between play and work. Harmony and conflict are incapable of being merged into some third entity, but must remain distinct. Nor can one become the other. It is equally clear that play and work are antagonistic. The spoilsport dampens the spirit of the gamesters, and the player runs the risk of doing violence to the orderly routine of the work world. Harmony and conflict are antagonistic, each being prone to destroy the other.

And yet, play and work are complementary. This is very important to understand, for workers and pseudo-players usually are aware of only the antagonism. In the saying, "All work and no play makes Jack a dull boy," the work world recognizes the necessity of play. The player recognizes the necessity of the work world. Unlike the pseudo-player who refuses to return to everyday living, he readily and joyfully returns to work with increased incentive. The true player knows that "All play and no work makes no Jack." Harmony and conflict are complementary, for conflict produces work that ensures survival, and harmony produces play that ensures the meaning and enjoyment of survival. Conflict alone is insufficient, because mere survival readily becomes so unenjoyable as to be self-defeating and ends in direct or indirect suicide. Harmony alone is equally insufficient, because mere enjoyment readily lessens the opportunity for survival and thus threatens the destruction of him who is able to enjoy. Therefore, our theory does not suggest the abolishment of work for the sake of play. The elimination of work would entail the elimination of man, and this would include the elimination of play. Work is almost a necessary evil, but not quite, for it does allow that survival which can be transformed into the state of play. The conclusion is that play and work are distinct, antagonistic, and complementary.

On the basis of this preliminary comparison, and from a psychological point of view, it is at least possible to suggest that the sacred is the realm of psychic harmony and the profane is the realm of psychic conflict. Thus an opening is made for a dynamic understanding of religion.

Ambivalence toward the Sacred. The most fundamental characteristic of man's experience of the sacred is the new awareness of what might be called *powerful form*. The use of two terms to describe this experience indicates that it is a single awareness that can be analyzed in two ways. Consideration of new form will be undertaken in the discussion of myth and ritual in the following chapter. Analysis of new power and man's ambivalent response to it is appropriate at this point.

Otto mentions the terms "overpoweringness," "energy," "urgency," and speaks of this energy as "a force that knows not stint nor stay, which is urgent, active, compelling, and alive."[8] The other historians mentioned previously agree, Van der Leeuw stating that experience of the sacred is the consequence of the *Power* it generates. He elaborates:

> We characterize the distance between the potent and the relatively powerless as the relationship between sacred and profane, or secular. The "sacred" is what has been placed within boundaries, the exceptional (Latin *sanctus*); its powerfulness creates for it a place of its own.[9]

Thus, the sacred is power, and whatever is not powerful is not a manifestation of the sacred. Whatever is powerless is of the profane.

One of the primitive concepts which signifies this power of the sacred and that has had great and frequently misleading influence on the study of primitive religion is the concept of *mana*. Codrington, the missionary who discovered the existence of this concept among the people of Melanesia, describes it as follows:

> The Melanesian mind is entirely possessed by the belief in a supernatural power or influence, called almost universally "mana." This is what works to effect everything which is

beyond the ordinary power of men, outside the common processes of nature; it is present in the atmosphere of life, attaches itself to persons and to things, and is manifested by results which can only be ascribed to its operation. When one has got it he can use it and direct it, but its force may break forth at some new point; the presence of it is ascertained by proof. A man comes by chance upon a stone which takes his fancy; its shape is singular, it is like something, it is certainly not a common stone, there must be mana in it. So he argues with himself, and he puts it to the proof; he lays it at the root of a tree to the fruit of which it has a certain resemblance, or he buries it in the ground when he plants his garden; an abundant crop on the tree or in the garden shows that he is right, the stone is mana, has that power in it. Having that power it is a ve-hicle to convey mana to other stones.[10]

Among the Melanesians the term always means power. According to Van der Leeuw the term suggests such ideas as "Influence, Strength, Fame, Majesty, Intelligence, Author-ity, Deity, Capability, extraordinary Power; whatever is suc-cessful, strong, plenteous: to reverence, be capable, to adore and to prophesy."[11] After this specific discovery, similar con-cepts were found the world over—the *orenda* of the Iroquois and the *wakanda* of the Sioux Indians, the *petara* of the Dy-aks of Borneo and the *megbe* of the African pygmies. These concepts and many others are not identical to mana, but are similar in the awareness of some sort of force that is power and makes things and people powerful. And even where a concept does not occur, there is still awareness of some vital power which impinges on man and is holy.

Perhaps the best analogy to the concepts which reflect this experience is that of electricity, a power which can be stored in a reservoir, transmitted through objects and people, which can help or hurt human beings, and which is difficult to control and does not always do what is expected. It can be noted that this awareness occurs in more developed religions, not only as the omnipotence of God, but also as the breath of the soul, the Greek *pneuma*. Now, it is not being asserted that all primitives have an identical concept with reference to experience of the sacred, nor that there is an early monistic stage in the history of religious thought. The concept of mana is used only to illustrate the awareness of power which is a constant in all experience of the sacred.

When it is understood that the sacred is manifest to man as power that breaks into his everyday world and is both antagonistic and yet complementary to this world, it is easy to appreciate man's mixed reactions to this experience. A second generalization as fundamental as that concerning the absolute distinction between sacred and profane is that primitive man responds *ambivalently* to sacred power. To be overwhelmed is not an event to which man reacts in any simple, straightforward fashion.

The ambivalence of man's response is the central theme of Otto's *The Idea of the Holy*. Man is considered to respond to the "numinous" as the *mysterium tremendum*. The first part of the term represents the element of "fascination" toward the "Wholly Other," and the latter part respresents the element of "awefulness." The positive element of "fascination" can be described rationally as issuing in love, mercy, pity, comfort, and in the wonderfulness, rapture, bliss, and grace that transcend all rational comprehension. The negative element of "awefulness" is described by the use of such terms as "grisly," "dread," "uncanny," "eerie," "weird," "shudder," and "horror." The awareness of the *mysterium tremendum* is given the following classic description:

> These two qualities, the daunting and the fascinating, now combine in a strange harmony of contrasts, and the resultant dual character of the numinous consciousness, to which the entire religious development bears witness, at any rate from the level of the "daemonic dread" onwards, is at once the strangest and most noteworthy phenomenon in the

whole history of religion. The daemonic-divine object may
appear to the mind an object of horror and dread, but at
the same time it is no less something that allures with a
potent charm, and the creature, who trembles before it, ut-
terly cowed and cast down, has always at the same time
the impulse to turn to it, nay even to make it somehow his
own. The "mystery" is for him not merely something to be
wondered at but something that entrances him; and beside
that in it which bewilders and confounds, he feels a something that captivates and transports him with a strange rav-
ishment, rising often enough to the pitch of dizzy intoxication; it is the Dionysiac-element in the numen.[12]

Van der Leeuw agrees with Otto, saying, with a different
use of the term, that primal "dread is essentially ambivalent,
a condition intermediate between being repelled and being
attracted."[13] Caillois writes that the sacred "constitutes the
supreme temptation and the greatest of dangers."[14] Eliade
affirms with regard to the relationship of primitive man and
the sacred:

> On the one hand he hopes to secure and strengthen his own
> reality by the most fruitful contact he can attain . . . ; on
> the other, he fears he may lose it completely if he is totally
> lifted to a plane of being higher than his natural profane
> state: he longs to go beyond it and yet cannot wholly leave
> it.[15]

Eliade notes that the ambivalence toward the sacred means
not only attraction and repulsion, but also the values of
"pure" and "impure." Caillois considerably expands this observation by stating that primitive societies do not differ-
entiate linguistically between a taboo that results from a
concern for sanctity and that which stems from a concern
for defilement, such terms as "tapu" and "pamali" designat-
ing what can be either blessed or accursed.[16] This does not
mean that there was an original identity of the pure and impure, but that the power of the sacred is not at all fixed like

an object. It is exceedingly mobile and capable of rendering good or evil, depending on the direction it takes. For example, a woman in childbirth is isolated from the group because of impurity, yet the milk of cows is brought to be touched by her in order to guarantee its purity. Whatever is pure under some conditions may be impure under others, and vice versa.

From these observations of the historians of religion, it can be concluded that the sacred is experienced as Power and that the response of primitive man is never neutral, but always similar to that described by Goethe in *The Fisher,* "Half drew she him, half sank he in." This response of primitive man is shared by all human beings to some degree. It is similar to the attitude of a child before the power of a fire—he wants to touch it, but is afraid of being burned. And fire for the adult contains the same polarity, for it both saves and destroys man. A stranger for primitive man, by the very fact of his strangeness and unexpectedness, was a manifestation of sacred power. The greeting given him was part of a religious ritual into which the power of the sacred was introduced to either repel or neutralize the alien power. Modern man's handling of strangers retains similar rituals for the identical reasons—both fear of, and attraction to, the power of the uncommon.

The more developed religions retain at least symbols of this awareness in the division of the sacred into positive and negative gods or spirits. There are God and the Devil, angels and demons, priests and sorcerers. But it is even more important to note that, despite this formal division into positive and negative beings and practices related to the sacred, the separate poles still provoke an ambivalent response. For the classical Christian, the sheer Evil of the Devil was not only fearful and tormenting, but also clearly enticing to the individual. And the Lord God who cherished man and promised him the Kingdom, remained fearful to behold and possessed of a wrath that could consume man and destroy his being. So even when the ambivalence issues into the vision of the sacred in polarity, the experience of the sacred remains thoroughly ambivalent.

The conclusion is that if man does not initially experience the sacred ambivalently, he is not really experiencing the sacred. If this understanding of the sacred and man's relationship to it is correct, and it is affirmed by at least every major historical religion, then a rather negative judgment follows about much of contemporary popular religion. That much of science fiction and other contemporary fantasy such as ghost stories arouses awareness of powerful ambivalence more than popular or even sophisticated writings on religion, suggests that the traditional faith has been severed from the experience which fostered it. Undoubtedly, the experience of the sacred and the ambivalence response continues, but it is not so easily related to the tradition.

According to our theory, the understanding of the sacred as power is related to the experience of psychic harmony. The work world of the profane is the realm of psychological conflict in which the need for discharge of energy is curtailed by inner warfare with the need for design. The individual worker experiences impotency. Transformation of the conflict into harmony enables the need for discharge to function fully, and so the individual experiences potency as a sudden and miraculous gift.

The ambivalence of man toward the sacred is also consistent with, and given dynamic understanding by, the theory of work and play. The sacred is fascinating because its appearance is necessary for the psychological fulfillment of the individual. Equilibrium is the inherent goal of an organism, and in the human being this includes that psychic harmony which creates the potentiality for adventure. The desire for a harmonious self is innate. But the ingrained longing for a new self and a new world is matched and frequently conquered by fear of loss and desire to preserve the old and conflicted self and its world. The sacred appears as "aweful" for at least two reasons.

First, the profane or work self is dedicated to the goal of minimizing risk and fostering routine. Its basic reaction to new experience is anxiety, for the breaking up of rigidity appears as chaos to the individual. Consequently, the manifestation of something different, even if it be a manifestation of harmony, is an occasion for dread. The second reason for this reaction lies in the conflicted self's interpretation of the sacred. The profane individual does not know the active peace of harmony, but the inactive peace that is stalemate. Likewise, with respect to the three other elements of play, he knows only the perversions and can only interpret the potentialities of the sacred accordingly. Thus, anything new is seen as more dangerous than what already is, and any possible change as a change for the worse. In this curious fashion, the response of awe toward the sacred reveals the deadliness of the profane. The profane is both powerless and hopeless. The conclusion is that the sacred necessarily appears fascinating to man because it is the sign of human fulfillment and that it almost inevitably appears awful because it is interpreted profanely as the sign of human destruction. The experience of power and the reaction of ambivalence are common to the sacred and to play because the dynamics underlying both are identical.

Secularity, Magic, and Religion. Experience of the sacred offers only potential for a religious response. The individual can flee from the sacred or misuse it, the results being not religion, but secularity or magic. The basic theme of the following analysis is that man's ambivalence toward the sacred is extremely difficult to maintain. The tension created is nearly unbearable, and release is sought. There are three possible "solutions" to the tension: flight into profane life by means of daily work; maintenance of the tension through the mingling of sacred and profane life by means of magic; and full entrance into sacred life by means of religion. The theory can be expressed simply. The appearance of the sacred is a manifestation of psychic harmony. When the response of awefulness rules over that of fascination, the result is a retreat to the profane in an attempt to ignore and forget the sacred. When the tension between awefulness and fascination remains, the result is the mingling of the sacred and profane in magic. And when the response of fascination rules over that of awefulness, the result is a full surrender of the work self and work world and entry into a new identity and new world that is called religious. We must consider these three alternatives with particular attention to magic because it is so common and yet so unrecognized. More will be said about what is not religion than about what is, due to the illusiveness of religion and the danger of perverting it.

The secular response occurs when awefulness rules over fascination in the experience of the sacred. This is the case for primitive man most of the time, and the sacred is experienced more as taboo than as festival. He labors to guard himself against the power of the sacred. Modern man seems to have gained more facility in this retreat and has created such effective taboos on the sacred that one can refer to desacralization. Rather than merely limit the sacred, he attempts to ignore it as completely as possible. Thus, Eliade speaks of the two "falls" of man:

> After the first "fall," the religious sense descended to the level of the "divided consciousness"; now, after the second, it has fallen even further, into the depths of the unconscious; it has been "forgotten."[17]

By this means, modern man attempts to ensure his precarious security in the world of work. The preceding discussions of the awefulness of the sacred and of the worker's fear of

psychic harmony and play were sufficient to explain this retreat. Religion is rare, not only because psychic harmony is
rare, but also because the rare presence of harmony is so
anxiety-provoking to the worker. Therefore, it can be said
that, contrary to the common assertion that religion is born
out of fear, it is secular life that is born out of fear—anxiety
over the holy.

It is important to realize that this "solution" to ambivalence cannot be completely successful. The primitive's daily
adherence to taboos was periodically broken into by the
festival that energetically sanctioned the breaking of sacred
prohibitions. In a similar fashion, although on a lower level,
modern man is continually plagued by a quasi-religious response to the sacred in spite of himself. No longer knowing
that he fundamentally desires awareness and acceptance of
the sacred, he falls into minor forms of worship. Eliade refers to the camouflaged myths, degenerated rituals, and the
use of literature and cinema for escape as examples of the
return to religion. The various forms of merrymaking that
accompany the New Year and other holidays, the festivities
related to personal events such as marriage and the birth of
a child, the other worlds of the past or future in fiction and
cinema, the little cults of the occult and spiritualism which
abound in the larger cities, and the competing ideologies of
the time—all these illustrate to some degree the return of
acceptance of the sacred.

And there is another whole area to be explored on this
matter. The denial of the sacred is the denial of the opportunity for full play, and the result is regression to partial
play. All the examples mentioned above are likely to occur
as partial play, as play that does not involve the total adult
personality. Thus, it is immature religion at best. This leads
to the observation that the modern trend away from the sacred is matched by increased participation in sports. What

has taken over the role of religion for an increasing number of modern men is the contemporary version of the Roman circus. Whether it be the drama and dance of the performing arts or the games of baseball and football, what are commonly known as leisure-time activities are becoming the current substitutes for religion. Modern man plays as a child plays rather than as an adult. This dynamic may, in part, explain the occasional negative reaction of the church to drama, dancing, and card playing. Certainly the church often has had a falsely serious orientation to religion, but it may also have had a genuine, if implicit, understanding that partial play was being used as a substitute for the full play of religion.

The conclusion is that fascination for the sacred is intrinsic to man and cannot be abolished. If an attempt is made to live secularly, the religious response will occur, although in a partial and regressive form. As rare as the saint who fully plays is the one who leads a profane life that is not implicitly and partially a religious response to the sacred.

The second possible outcome of initial ambivalence toward the sacred is the response of magic. This is the most common "solution" and the most difficult to understand, for magic is the attempt to achieve the impossible—the mingling of the sacred and the profane. Before analyzing this phenomenon, it is useful to consider the contributions of the historians of religion.

According to Rudolf Otto, the manifestation of magic requires two elements—the sacred and man's attempt to manipulate it. Magic is only possible because of the element of the numinous. Noting that the modern bowler's body moves in accordance with his desire to have the ball correctly placed at the other end of the alley, he suggests that such action is not magical, but only "naïvely analogical." He refers to the conception of mountains and other natural objects

as animate and concludes that even such awareness in itself
does not imply awareness of the sacred:

> The objects in question only become "divine"—objects of
> worship—when the category of the numinous is applied to
> them, and that does not come about until, first, an attempt
> is made to *influence* them by numinous means, viz., by
> magic; and, second, their special efficacy or way of work-
> ing is at the same time accepted as something numinous,
> viz., something magical.[18]

Now it is highly questionable that magic is a form of "pre-
religion" as Otto suggests and that objects are not perceived
as numinous until an attempt is made to use them. Such a
view of the history of man's reaction to the sacred was once
fashionable and no doubt a comfort to modern man because
it put magic in the distant past, but it is not upheld by
anthropological studies. Yet the basic point of Otto is sound:
Magic requires both awareness of the sacred and the attempt
to manipulate it. His conclusion is that *magic is the attempt
to control the sacred.*

It is the contribution of Van der Leeuw that most fully
develops the theme of Otto. Magic is defined by the former
as the "autocratic seizure of power."[19] Rather than being
marked by the humility of the religious person, the magician
possesses the arrogance that the Greeks called *hubris* and
the Hindus illustrated in the belief that ascetic practices
make the throne of the divine hot. Van der Leeuw comments
on this point:

> He who thus assumes the magical attitude . . . resembles
> the conductor dominating his orchestra; and it may well be
> that he believes that he himself produces the uproar. . . .
> In magic, then, the dictum *eritis sicut Deus*—"ye shall be as
> gods"—attains full reality. . . .[20]

Magic is seen by Van der Leeuw as being a *protest* in

which the individual says "nevertheless" and proceeds to fashion his own world by imitating the divine power of creation. If a primitive man violates a prohibition by stepping over another person, he can nullify the action simply by stepping over once more in the reverse direction. Likewise, the little modern child can avoid stepping on cracks in the sidewalk on the way home from school to ensure that such an improbable event as receiving mail will occur. By magic, what happens can be nullified and what does not happen can be required to happen. However, the way of magic is deemed to have one essential condition: autism. Before the world can be controlled magically, it must be transferred inward and the consequence is a "living with oneself." The primitive may receive status in a community that is like-minded, but the modern magician often is termed insane. The magical attitude is illustrated by the megalomania of the schizophrenic who refers to himself as divine or who falls out of bed in order to keep the earth rotating.

Van der Leeuw carefully points out that religion and magic cannot be separated "as though religion were the successor of magic, the latter being non-religious and the former never magical."[21] Magic deals with the sacred, and some "religions" seek to dominate and control the sacred. Magic is not just a primitive science or a precursor of science that modern man has outgrown, but a fundamental response that will occur as long as man experiences the sacred. The mania to dominate the world by use of the sacred power is inherent in man and therefore present in *all* men:

> This magical attitude, however, is not a structure of the spiritual life merely of the past, of which only meagre vestiges now persist for us; nor, again, is it a degeneration nor childish malady; it is neither "primitive science" nor elementary technique. It is, on the contrary, a primal attitude very deeply grounded in human nature, as vital among ourselves as it ever was, in fact an eternal structure.[22]

Thus, the magical attitude is considered to be the seizure of sacred power in protest and the autistic creation of a new world that ultimately ends in insanity for the modern man. The yearning of Goethe's Faust is understandable:

> Could I my pathway but from magic free,
> And quite unlearn the spells of sorcery,
> Stood I, Oh Nature, man alone 'fore thee,
> Then were it worth the trouble man to be![23]

Now it is appropriate to analyze magic as an attempt to achieve the impossible—mingling the sacred and the profane. The basic point is that the magician, rather than responding religiously to the sacred by playing, responds profanely by working. Primitive man becomes aware of the sacred as a manifestation of power and reacts ambivalently with fascination and awe. A predominance of the former leads to participation in religion; a predominance of the latter leads to escape to the profane; and a predominance of neither leads to the performance of magic. Fascination prevents flight to the profane and awe prevents participation in religion, so the only possible result is that profane use of the sacred which is magic. Following the theory of work and play, it can be said that the magician is one who experiences new energy, is fascinated because such power betokens the fulfillment of himself. Yet he is also fearful because it threatens his already anxious life and is falsely interpreted by the conflicted profane self, and so is impelled neither to accept nor deny psychic harmony, but to attempt to work with it. Thus magic is neither profane nor religious; it is an antireligious response to the sacred.

It is no wonder that modern secular man has responded to "religion" as a crutch for combating fear, for it has been such on the whole, namely, magic. A truly religious response to the sacred has remained the rare achievement of a few individuals. The worker is most distinguishable from the player by the presence of anxiety, the leading characteristic of the magician. Bronislaw Malinowski gives this analysis:

> Magic is to be expected and generally to be found when-
> ever man comes to an unbridgeable gap, a hiatus in his
> knowledge or in his powers of practical control, and yet has
> to continue in his pursuit. Forsaken by his knowledge, baf-
> fled by the results of his experience, unable to apply an
> effective technical skill, he realizes his impotence. Yet his
> desire grips him only the more strongly. His fears and
> hopes, his general anxiety, produce a state of unstable equi-
> librium in his organism, by which he is driven to some sort
> of vicarious activity.[24]

When a primitive tiller of the soil has worked as hard as he can to care for his fields, the coming of a drought may over-whelm him. The threat to his survival is responded to with magical rites to insure success of the crops. When man can-not accomplish what he wants to accomplish, anxiety occurs. Under these conditions, magical charms, spells, and rites are created in an attempt to get what cannot be gotten by every-day work. Finally, he becomes so attached to the rituals of magic that failure to perform them or incorrect performance also gives rise to anxiety. The magician is the most fearful of all human beings, for both the profane and the sacred make him anxious.

What is most curious about magic is its persistence, since being a mingling of the sacred and profane, it is an attempt at an impossibility. We have emphasized that the sacred and the profane are distinct and antagonistic; if they are mingled, either the sacred or the profane is destroyed. So, although the most common, magic is the least viable of the three possible reactions to ambivalence toward the sacred.

On the one hand, magical practices may slowly destroy the sacred and turn it into profane routine that vaguely re-calls the sacred rite. Van der Leeuw suggests that "habit"

becomes an inner attitude in which there is neither blessed-
ness nor damnation. He adds:

> But as regards the "Wholly Other," habit is always very
> foolish: In three days, just when the horse became used to
> eating nothing at all, it died; and when man has completely
> lost his capacity for surprise, he too is as good as dead![25]

In this case, a magical response flees the sacred and becomes
purely profane. Defense against anxiety caused by the sacred
rules.

On the other hand, magical practices may destroy the
profane, and with it, the sanity of the individual. The magician is quite right to fear and protect himself against the
sacred. He is exposed to the possibility of having his profane
world destroyed and at the same time is incapable of allowing
a new sacred world to be created. This is the basic source of
his anxiety. To live in such a state has been known as damnation and is now known as insanity. Modern profane man
has forgotten what primitive man knew very well: the sacred
can destroy human personality. Such damnation can occur
in the social as well as the individual realm. It has been suggested that the modern replacement for the sacred festival
is war.[26] Like the primitive festival, modern war is the result
of a society's search for renewal of life; unlike the festival, it
profoundly fails in this attempt. Modern war is man's magical
seizure of the sacred, and it results in the destruction of man
by the sacred. Magic is an attempt at an impossibility and
must necessarily end in the chronic dying of the profane
man or in the cataclysmic death of the psychotic individual
or society.

It should be apparent that the magician does not experience the elements of play—peace, freedom, delight, and
illusion. What appears similar to these elements can only
be perversions of play. There is no peace, but only conflict
within. Profane conflict rules his response and is merely

underground to visit with the spirits of the dead and ascends to the heavens to gain wisdom from the divine spirits. The very gods travel to create and sustain the world. Not only Abraham, but all religious individuals are called to leave their home in the profane and travel into that apparent wilderness of the sacred. And not to understand the recorded life of Jesus as a tale of adventure is perverse piety. No religious person has a place to lay his head in the profane, but rests in the excitement of the sacred, full of both harmony and power.

To be filled with harmony and power is to experience the elements of peace, freedom, delight, and illusion. While neither the secular man nor the magician possesses peace, the religious man receives this gift. This is the inner peace, that is, peace between man and the sacred, which enables him to accept the conflict which occurs without and participate in it in an adventuresome way. There is freedom, because acceptance of the new power grants power to the individual. The irony is that the religious man truly receives the power the magician desires. But he receives it only because he uses it not for his own secular ends but for the sake of adventure itself. In the absence of anxiety, there is delight which knows no defeat despite all conflict which rages in the world. And in the illusion of the religious man, there is not psychosis, but full awareness of two worlds which prevents profane madness and allows only the sacred madness of the adventurer.

The religious man is acknowledged by the primitive as a sacred person, as one who has been touched by sacred power. And their reaction to the earliest professionals of the sacred is ambivalence. The religious person is responded to just as is the sacred with both fascination and awefulness. He beckons his fellow men toward another life and they are attracted and yet repelled. The holy men of all ages and traditions are the ultimate authorities for their societies, but may be called

upon only as a last resort because of their dangerous qualities. Thus, to be religious is to be like the sacred, to be
powerful and yet responded to ambivalently by the workers,
fled by some and used magically by others. This is the inevitable martyrdom which occurs in all who offer the religious
response to the sacred. But the religious martyr is at full
play and receives all the gifts of play. So, despite the common misunderstanding of the workers about martyrdom, it
is the case that only the religious martyr makes merry. What
is more dumfounding to most members of Western society
than those who were Christian martyrs in the early Church?
Their joy is so bizarre to modern secular man that he either
denies the joy or labels them psychotic. Yet they do not so
frequently dismiss the adventurer who climbs Mt. Everest or
sails the Atlantic in a small sailing craft. What is acknowledged on lesser levels is denied on the highest level. The
adventure of the religious man is too much for secular man
to behold.

The fundamental point being made is that there is a difference between the secular or magical man and the religious
man. Traditional societies, even though perhaps somewhat
more accustomed to the sacred than modern man, possessed
a clear understanding that the holy man was different. For
contemporary man, the difference might be even more striking to the beholder and might also be even more difficult to
tolerate. The player's piety is not conventional. The conventional Christian, and this is at least partly every Christian most of the time, is not religious. This is to say that the
Christian, for example, who feels overwhelmed by conflict
within or without himself, or who feels weighted down by
responsibility to God and his neighbor, or who lives his life
with a perpetual frown, or who has no awareness of a new
being and a new world—this man is not religious. Either he
has not met God, or he has met and is fleeing him, or he has
met and is manipulating him. The alternatives to the reli-

gious response to the sacred cover a great deal of territory.

Finally, it can be repeated that as the child does not play continually and does no work, neither does the religious man. He does not forever abandon the profane, but continually returns to the problems of the work world. Even in the presumed world-denying Orient, the most favored of the holy work in the profane world. The story is told of four men who discovered a place enclosed by a high wall and were determined to see what was inside. They found a ladder and scaled the wall one by one. The first ascended the ladder, looked over the top of the wall, and then jumped in with joyous laughter. The second and the third did the same. When the fourth and last man got to the top of the wall, he saw the garden of his dreams. But he did not follow the others. Rather, he returned to his countrymen to tell them about the beautiful garden. The Indian tale illustrates the way of the religious man. He returns to "labor" for those who know nothing but labor. Because of this return to the profane, the conflicted self regains control of the individual to some extent, but memory of the harmonious self inspires it to try to understand and guide all who live profane lives. The religious man alternates between play for its own sake and work for the sake of his fellow men. And this work is closer to play than it is to the work of the profane man because it is not work for oneself. It is this dynamic of the religious man that is so inexplicable to the secular man and magical man. They seek to hang on to what little pleasures they have. But the player knows that adventures are not continuous. And, having had an adventure, he is grateful about it and eager to share his experience.

Because of this dialectic of sacred and profane in the life of the religious man, both sacred and profane are acknowledged and their relationship maintained as distinct, antagonistic, and yet complementary. Therefore, the religious response is the only real solution to ambivalence toward the sacred. Without both worlds being acknowledged as complementary, there is only destruction of the individual; with acknowledgment, there is mature adventure. The most uncommon and yet only viable response to the sacred is to play fully; this is the gift to the person who is genuinely religious.

It can be noted in conclusion that none of the three possible responses to the sacred is necessarily easily identifiable. He who is labeled by modern man as a primitive sorcerer might well have been more concerned about sheer participation in the sacred than the attempt to manipulate it; likewise, the seemingly religious person might well have been devoutly intent on seizing divine power for his own use. Further, primitive man is no longer considered to have been as completely captured by the magic-religious response as was once thought by earlier historians of religion, and modern man is surely not so secular as he may like to imagine. Thus, an understanding of the basic dynamics of play and work as revealed in the sacred and the profane is not sufficient for analyzing specific responses. What is required is application of these dynamics of play to the modes of myth and ritual. By this means some of the more specific elements of religion, magic, and the secular can be described.

5 Play, Myth, and Ritual ....

OUR DISCUSSION of religion, magic, and the secular in relation to the sacred was limited in value because the sacred is never encountered purely as power. It is manifested by means of objects and persons, or, better, it is an event in which the individual is confronted with power in a relationship to objects and persons. The sacred is present in a stone, tree, star, or building; in a leader, murderer, secret society, or conquering tribe. The sacred is always manifest as form as well as power; awareness of the sacred is awareness of *powerful form*. As our theory posits, psychic harmony leads to full design of experience as well as to full discharge of energy.

The adventure of the mature adult that issues from inner harmony is acknowledged by tradition as myth and ritual. It was concluded previously that a play adventure occurs in the modes of story and game and that these modes are compatible, inseparable, and finally one in the living of an adventure. One mode may be more clearly revealed to the observer, but the other will never be entirely absent. The story told by the mature adventurer is a myth, and the game he plays is a ritual. All that was concluded about the nature of story and games applies to the nature of myth and ritual. And this includes the fact of the inseparability of the two modes. It cannot be overemphasized that myth and ritual are only useful abstractions from a single reality—mature adventure. The full living out of myth creates a ritualistic life, and the full living out of ritual creates a mythical life. Because some modern students of religion seem to divide this response to the sacred into myth and ritual only in order to ignore one or the other, or to argue that one or the other has historical primacy, a preliminary discussion of the indivisibility is appropriate.

There was a tendency among nineteenth-century students of religion to study mythology in isolation from ritual. Indeed, the study tended to be in isolation from culture as a whole. There was little attempt to understand the relation of myth to daily behavior, ritual or otherwise.[1] This limited approach was probably dissipated by the increasing contributions of anthropologists in the field who clearly demonstrated that myth and ritual tend to be highly interdependent. But wide variation does occur. In classical Greece, there are many myths about the Area, but few rituals connected with them. The early Roman seemed to place more emphasis on ritual than on myth. The Bushmen had many myths and little ritual. And among the Papago, some myths seem to have no ceremonial enactment, while some rituals have content foreign to the myths. In a sense, almost any theory about the relationship of the two modes can be validated and yet be limited. But the most general valid conclusion seems to be that myth and ritual tend to be related and that either can be predominant in a given culture. Their universal association cannot be doubted.

In the twentieth century, there has been a movement to establish one mode as prior to, and the source of, the other. The emphasis now is upon ritual and its priority over myth. Students of the religion of the Near East point out that myths are used to explain and justify rituals. It is concluded that ritual is primary and that myth dies when separated from it.[2] This conclusion cannot be supported by comprehensive data. Kluckhohn challenges it by reference to studies of the Navaho.[3] It is acknowledged that all ritual practice is justified by an accompanying myth in this culture. And it is also true that a practitioner may carry out a ritual chant without even knowing the story related to it. These instances would support the theory of the primacy of ritual. But there are data that point to the opposite conclusion. One Navaho "priest" was a transvestite who changed current myths in order to make a hermaphrodite god the supreme deity, contrary to the tradition. Kluckhohn notes that other Navahos said that some rituals were revised to be in accord with this new mythical focus. This is an example of a myth coming before and influencing ritual. It is also noted that one practitioner created a new ritual which he had learned in a dream and that tradition states that many myths come from such dreams or visions. This is not to say that dreams cause myths and myths cause ritual, for ritual can surely influence the dreamer. But the simple conclusion that rituals are the source of myth inevitably is not upheld. If it is the case that some myths justify rituals and appear after the occurence of rituals, and that some new myths have given rise to new rituals, no theory can stress only one side of the matter. The only fair generalization is that myth and ritual are intimately associated and influence each other.

It is not our purpose to add any light to the current debate on the relationship of myth and ritual in primitive culture. The focus is more on the individual and on a psychological understanding of the two modes. It may well be that the mode of game appears in the individual child earlier than the mode of story. This would follow from what is known about individual development. We will focus, however, on the adult who possesses the potential for both game and story. And the theory is that the story that is fully one's own story is told by more than merely verbal behavior. When the telling of a story involves the total personality, the result is a game. And when ritual is observed by the total personality, the result is a myth in dramatic form. So myth is told by living as well as by speaking, and ritual is a way of living as well as an occasional performance. In addition, it can be suggested that, in either the individual or the culture as a whole, separation of the two modes could be destructive of both. Acceptance of a story that does not include change of behavior is not really acceptance. Performance of ritual that is not grounded in story is not really performance, but only going through the motions. At the simplest level, there can be no separation, for full speech leads to body movement and body movement evokes speech. At the more complicated level, there should be no fundamental conflict between prophet and priest, for unless one includes the other, neither can exist. In the terminology of this essay, myth and ritual are modes of adventure, and an adventure is *meaningful and graceful action.* The conclusion is that the goal of the individual and of the culture is full and equal expression of play adventure in both modes. This follows from the basic dynamics of play. Psychic harmony leads to full design of experience, and this includes full play in both modes.

The following discussion of play, myth, and ritual will offer a very limited sampling of a vast literature in order to illustrate and deepen understanding of the religious, magical, and secular responses to the sacred. Special attention will be given to the problems of time and belief in relation to myth, and to space and sacrifice in relation to ritual. Consideration of these problems in the light of responses to the sacred may make the equation of play and religion more comprehensible and useful to modern man.

Myth. It is common for the modern intellectual to state that a myth at its best is creative fiction, and at its worst,

sheer superstition. What he means by "fiction" and "superstition" is not always very clear. Myth tends to be regarded
as an outmoded form of thinking that is attractive in its
fancies, but replaced by more scientific thinking. But the
universal understanding of myth was quite different. At its
very best, a myth is a matter of superstition in the classical
Latin sense of the term—as a "witnessing" or "standing over."
"Superstition" implies an experience of transcendence, and
it is this peculiar awareness of the "beyond" that is so in-
furiating to modern man. We prefer to hide from the experience of the "Other" by erecting a screen of philosophical,
scientific, and theological terminology, but that which is
other will remain other.

Because of this contemporary bias wherein "myth" is commonly used in the pejorative sense, this discussion begins
with a summary of the meaning of myth for the primitive as
interpreted by a historian of religion. Of the authorities previously mentioned, Eliade offers the most comprehensive
understanding. This statement is followed by an analysis
with special attention to the problems of time and belief.

Eliade's contribution is summarized in one of his latest
works, *Myth and Reality*. His basic understanding is presented in this compact and complicated sentence:

> In general it can be said that myth as experienced by ar-
> chaic societies, (1) constitutes the History of the acts of the
> Supernaturals; (2) that this History is considered to be ab-
> solutely *true* (because it is concerned with realities) and
> *sacred* (because it is the work of the Supernaturals); (3)
> that myth is always related to a "creation," it tells how
> something came into existence, or how a pattern of behav-
> ior, an institution, a manner of working were established;
> this is why myths constitute the paradigms of all signifi-
> cant human acts; (4) that by knowing the myth one knows
> the "origin" of things and hence can control and manipu-
> late them at will; this is not an "external," "abstract" knowl-

edge but a knowledge that one "experiences" ritually, either by ceremonially recounting the myth or by performing the ritual for which it is the justification; (5) that in one way or another one "lives" the myth, in the sense that one is seized by the sacred, exalting power of the events recollected or re-enacted.[4]

It is noteworthy that the first three of the five points are related to time, and this is the focus of the following discussion. The fourth point will be considered under the analysis of the magical use of myth. The final point concerning seizure by the sacred and living out a myth has already been considered.

Eliade's understanding of myth focuses on the meaning of sacred and profane time. Profane time is continuous and irreversible, whereas sacred time is an interruption into temporal duration and is reversible. Myth tells what happened in the beginning, how existence came into being. By "history" Eliade does not mean what is "historic" to modern man, but what "consists solely of the mythical events which took place *in illo tempore* and have been unceasingly repeated from that day to this."[5] The manifestation of the sacred in myth serves to make primordial time present to the individual.

Sacred time may be manifest in both periodic and non-periodic events. Actions such as hunting and fishing may appear to be profane, but frequently are a sacred imitation of the primal acts of the gods, that is, a physical telling of the story. Any time may become a sacred time, and Eliade concludes that the sacred may be experienced independently of any ritual systems based on the framework of social life. As a periodic event, sacred time occurs in all the rites and festivals of the community, both those which concern the crises of the group and those which conform to seasonal change. In all such cases, as the myth is told and acted out, the individual lives in the sacred time of the beginnings.

Eliade lays stress in his recent work on the end of "history" as well as on the beginning. In a sense, the primitive view is that the end has already occurred, although it will be repeated in the future.[6] But the most important thing to note about the end is that it is also a beginning. The chaos of the end is only a prelude to a new creation. Therefore, the myth of the end and the myth of the beginning are identical, and any participation in sacred time is a repetition of the god's transformation of chaos into a World.

To claim that primitive man considered myth to be "true" means that "myth expresses in action and drama what metaphysics and theology define dialectically!"[7] Myth is "true" because, as has been frequently observed, it explains why things are as they are. More dynamically, it can be said that myth is "true" because man can do only what the gods have done before him. Unless one is initiated and given sacred knowledge of what the gods did, he is unable to perform as an adult human being. Finally, myth is "true" because the sacred is more "real" than the profane. The profane is what is not truly established by the gods, has no model, is vain, illusory, and "ontologically" unreal.[8]

It should be noted that not all the stories told by primitive man possess this reality. Van der Leeuw refers to the saga, fairy tale, and legend. The saga is defined as a myth that has become related to a specific historical fact, referring wholly to the past, eliminating the present quality of myth, and inspiring only a contemplative attitude.[9] The fairy tale is considered to be closer to myth, as it remains apart from the everyday world and is of great significance in the magical achievement of survival. And the legend is of less significance because the stories of the saints lack sacred power and offer little more than pious edification. Eliade reports that primitives distinguish between "true" and "false" stories. Making the same point as Van der Leeuw, he states that "true" stories, first of all, include those relating to the beginnings of the world and are peopled with divine actors; next,

stories of the exploits of a cultural hero who saved his people; and, finally, stories concerning the origin and power
of the medicine man.[10] The "false" stories include humorous
fables and tales about animals and men which can be told
on any occasion independently of sacred ritual. Eliade concludes that the basic difference between true stories and
false stories for primitive man is as follows:

> . . . everything that myths related *concerns them directly*,
> while the tales and fables refer to events that, even when
> they have caused changes in the World (cf. the anatomical
> or physiological peculiarities of certain animals), have not
> altered the human condition as such.[11]

In sum, Eliade believes that the goal of primitive man is
to kill time, that is, to destroy profane time and live in the
"eternal." This is what is meant by the desire to "live" a
myth. Existence degenerates and becomes old, so it must be
periodically renewed. The understanding behind the festival
is that there was perfection in the beginning that the flux
of time laid waste, so the old must be destroyed in a breach-
ing of all the normal patterns of society, and the original
creation of the world must be repeated. If the primitive man
were to speak through the mind of Eliade, he would perhaps
say:

> If we pay no attention to it, time does not exist; further-
> more, where it becomes perceptible—because of man's "sins,"
> i.e., when man departs from the archetype and falls into
> duration—time can be annulled.[12]

A way to put some flesh on the abstract bones of Eliade's
conclusions is to consider a story about creation told by the
Thompson Indians on the West Coast.[13] It is said that the
Stars, Moon, Sun, and Earth all lived together before the
world was created. Earth was a woman married to the Sun.
She constantly found fault with him, scolding him and saying that he was too hot. Finally the Sun left her and the

Moon and Stars went away with him. Earth-Woman was very sad. Then the Old One appeared and turned these people into their present form. He assigned Sun, Moon, and Stars to the sky and forbade them ever to desert the Earth again. Earth-Woman became the solid land. "You will be as the mother of people, for from you their bodies will spring, and to you they will go back. People will live as in your bosom, and sleep on your lap. They will derive nourishment from you, and they will utilize all parts of your body." Then the Earth gave birth to people. At first they had no desires or thoughts, but the Old One visited them and gave them these. He created animals, gave them names, and assigned them functions. He taught women how to gather food and make things. He taught men how to make fire and catch fish. And he taught men and women how to have intercourse and give birth to children. When he had finished all these things, he left the people, saying: "I now leave you; but if you . . . require my aid, I will come again to you. The Sun is your father, the Earth is your mother's body. You will be covered with her flesh as a blanket, under which your bones will rest in peace."

The story is about beginnings and informs the hearer about the creation of much that concerns human beings: stars, sun, moon, earth, plants, animals, and human beings themselves. The hearer discovers why animals, men, and women do what they do, why man is able to survive and how he will be protected even in death. By Eliade's definition, such a story is neither a saga, fairy tale, nor legend, but a story of ultimate concern to the people—a myth. It fulfills the formal requirements, being a history of the acts of sacred beings which tells about creation.

Now what would it be like to tell and hear this story as a myth? During such a moment, the story would not be considered as creative fiction or as sheer superstition, but as the "truth." This would not be expressed in any abstract fashion. Indeed, the question of "truth" would only puzzle the one to whom it is raised, and he would reply, as Eskimos do, "It is so because it is said that it is so."[14] This is what can be said and only what can be said, and it is really saying nothing at all. That is, nothing is said to convince the outsider. To be fully possessed by this story for a moment would be to exist in another world and in another time when existence is powerful, orderly, and fresh. With total absence of aesthetic appreciation and scientific skepticism, "knowledge" and experience of the Sun as our father and the Earth as our mother would grant the unspoken awareness that the World is our home, even in the midst of the profane, suffering and death. So, to live in the sacred time of the myth is really to live.

The general perspective added to the conclusions of Eliade should be apparent. Since a myth is a story, its source is the harmony of the needs for discharge of energy and design of experience which issues in adventure. Full mature play creates the type of story defined as myth. As stated previously, a story has a beginning and an end, and the two are related. Experience is designed and therefore significant to the individual. Without awareness of beginnings and endings, there is only awareness of chaos. Primitive man clearly understood the profane as the chaotic as well as the powerless. The world of conflict and of work to overcome it is without beginning or end, not only ineffective, but also insignificant. Without a plot, there is neither *significant identity* nor *meaningful action*. So the profane is experienced as either random or routine activity, each disturbing the other. A life of compulsive routine occasionally deranged by impulsive chaos is a life of anxiety. It is clear that primitive man took no such delight in the secular as modern man appears to. Rather, he preferred to be an *actor* in the drama which overcame both the chaos and routine of the profane life.

Eliade is correct in saying that the form of the story reflects the depth of the individual's existence, and Van der Leeuw also expresses the truth in the judgment that the saga, fairy tale, and legend are related to the sacred. The different forms of the story reflect the development of play in the individual and the existence of partial play. What are called the "true" stories or myths are those which reflect the fundamental concerns of the mature human being. Such a person is open to discover answers to the questions: "How did I come to be?", "Who am I?", and "Where am I going?" All other stories are the product of partial play, which is immature; the fairy tales reflect the limited play of the child, and the sagas reflect youth's identification with the hero. The difference between myth and other stories is the difference between full and partial play. This is not to say that the "false" stories are to be discarded, for primitive man evidently concluded otherwise. These smaller stories are included in, and oriented about, the big stories. What happens is that the leading story gathers about it the other stories and gives them a focus. What happens in a culture also occurs in the individual. Each person has many little stories which reflect various aspects of his life. These stories are put into perspective by the big story. It is the latter which validates them and gives them meaning and significance.

This rather natural approach to stories is what makes the conclusions of modern man seem so bizarre. If he considers himself "religious," he is apt to dismiss the other stories from other cultures and even from his own society and his own personal life. The big story is disconnected from the others. Owing to the fact that one story has always gathered others about it, it may be at least suspected that the big story is not really being accepted as a story. Indeed, what appears in cold print as obvious—that a myth is a story to be participated in —is not at all obvious to modern man. A Christian who does not have his story connected to the smaller stories of his family life and vocational life is likely to be either protecting his story or protecting himself from the story. In neither case does he participate in it. On the other hand, if modern man considers himself "secular," he is apt to dismiss the most mature story and accept the smaller, "false" ones. Fairy tales, legends, and sagas rule or misrule his life, and this amounts to only partial play at best. Typically, the family or the vocation becomes the ruling story. And when children leave home, a spouse dies, a business fails, or retirement is enforced, the size of the story becomes all too clear. So the "true" stories for modern man are either isolated or ignored, and it is probable that the latter frequently follows the former.

The full adventure that is lived and communicated as myth is basically connected with time, for sacred time is story time. The nature of this time can best be appreciated by considering first the nature of secular time and magical time.

The nature of the profane experience of time depends on which of the basic needs is in ascendance. The need for discharge of energy itself knows no time, functions without reminiscence or anticipation, and can be said to live in eternity. Indeed, when this need fully rules over the need for design, the result is a mystical experience of timelessness. There is a basic connection between the traditional experience of mysticism and the contemporary experience of pleasure. Indeed, the two are identical and the attraction of drugs for "transcendence" to the pleasure-seeking youth of our time is perfectly logical. The "be-ins" of the youth and the experience of the mystic are one, except in the matter of degree. In both cases, the need for discharge rules for a moment, and in both cases the need for design is impaired with the consequence of a "dark night of the soul" or, in modern terms, psychotic disorientation.

The need for design of experience knows time as chronological, as a passage measured by perception of change, for example, the movement of the heavens and the growth and decay of plants. When this need fully rules, the result is awareness of change. But, whereas the primitive gained his awareness from seasons, moon, sun, and plants, modern man is more precise in his awareness due to the invention and use of the clock. It is neither star time nor plant time that informs man, but clock time. The fascination of the clock for man is explained by the need for design of experience. Time can be ordered and controlled precisely. Rather than knowing just the morning, afternoon, evening, and night of the primitive, or the twelve hours of the ancients, modern man can know minutes and seconds. The bells of the monastery and whistles of the factory have been superseded by minute and second hands. It is not only the mother who tells her child to "Come here this second," but also the executives in modern industry. Change now is perceived as occurring by the second, and every second is important, because the change can work for or against "progress." As de Grazia points out, the clock's main function is to give signals so that human beings can start and stop activities together.[15] The result is "hourly rate" and "piece rate," spending time and buying time, and most of all, being on time—an hour means sixty minutes and 2:10 means just that. Biological time has been replaced by clock time. When the need for design of experience rules, the awareness is of change, and for contemporary man, the change is constant, rapid, and precise.

Generally, the needs for discharge of energy and design of experience are in conflict and time is burdensome. In this case, the need for discharge is discontented with regulation, and the need for design fearful of interruption. Eternity is threatened by routine, and time is threatened by dissolution. Profane history is duration or time, occasionally broken up by eternity, but never given significance. So modern man can be seen as divided into two types—the "hippies" who waste time and flee time, and the "businessmen" who save

time and seek time. But the war also occurs within each individual, for neither approach grants significant and meaningful time. Consequently, when that harmony occurs which
offers opportunity for adventure and story and the ambivalent response becomes ruled by awefulness, the result is
flight back into the conflicted attitude toward time of the
secular life. The secular response to myth is little more than
endurance of chronological time and timelessness with little
enjoyment of either. Because man is possessed by both fundamental needs, he may seek release from one kind of time
only to seek release then from the other.

The magical response to myth occurs when the initial
ambivalence toward the sacred is maintained. The sacred is
manipulated by the profane for the sake of survival. The
worker is anxious about his life. What he desires is *more
time,* and he perceives the sacred as a way of getting it.
Profane time as duration is all he knows. It does not live
up to his expectations, but he has no awareness of another
kind of time, so he desires more of the same. He uses the
sacred in the hope of achieving the two classic desires of
apparent "religion"—long life and everlasting life. The focus
is on quantity rather than quality. Characteristically, the
magician is greedy for more of what he does not enjoy in
the first place. So the primitives venerated those who attained a great many years, and man has always sought foun-
tains of youth. The classical "religious" man envisioned the
afterlife as a continued duration—immortality, and man
continues this belief in spiritualistic cults and popular religion. The desire for simple duration in another life is the
common desire of the magician, and such people are obviously exceedingly extant. The fact that all the traditional
religions center their attention on death and survival suggests that a magical understanding of time is the most abundant of the three possible responses to the sacred.

It should be realized that such a response is apparent in

the supposed profanity of contemporary man. To some extent the medical practitioner has replaced the magical priest. The concern for youth and health is apparent. The gobbling of vitamin pills and swallowing of noncaloric soft drinks is a combination which could make sense only to contemporary man. And, most significantly, the ambivalence of society toward the medical profession seems equal to that of primitive society to the medicine man. Doctors are responded to as priests, considered suspiciously, derogated, or ignored (to the extent of not paying bills) when their assistance is not required, but submitted to with great awe and obedience when survival is threatened. The story of modern man and medicine differs in no significant degree from the story of primitive man. Survival is still the goal of life, and illness and death the greatest threat. Modern man is thus a magician with respect to time. Nothing is more characteristic of modern man than the complaint, "If I only had more time," and that he might achieve more of it through his God is his "religious" desire. But the end result, at best, is that world weariness common to the ancient Hindus and contemporary aged which allows pleasure in the release from time. Modern man discovers what primitive man knew—that existence runs down. Profane time makes one tired. So the magician finally becomes secular and then desires release from the chains of time.

The religious response to the sacred grants the participant a new kind of time. The appearance of a story marks the transformation of duration by eternity, neither remaining as it is, but each being transformed into a single awareness of a powerful and significant time. Having its source in both new energy and new design, sacred time is an adventuresome time. The ideal full player lives a narrative existence that removes him from both the desperate holding on to the duration of clock time and desperate flight into the pleasures of eternity. He remains in the everyday world, but with a

new form of time. Nor does he seek more and more time as
the magician does. Whereas the magician is never satisfied
with the accumulation of time, the full player is satisfied
with each moment of his time. When time is actually significant for the individual, a moment is complete in and of
itself and more time is not required. He lives "at the end of
time." As has been stated repeatedly, survival is not an issue.
Time, that is, profane time, has been fulfilled for the adventurer. Now, it may appear to the profane individual that
"once upon a time" or "at the end of time" is "no time."
This is undoubtedly a cause of "religious" concepts of eternity. But if the sacred is always manifest as a story and plot,
it is apparent that some kind of time is involved. There can
be no plot in eternity. This is the vain and ultimately boring
dream of the pleasure seeker. The religious man, on the contrary, anticipates adventure. It is the "once upon a time"
and "at the end of time" of the mature adventurer which
brings the new time which is not only characterized by the
element of illusion, but by the elements of peace, freedom,
and delight as well. What would it be like to live with no
fear of time, no fear of timelessness, and no need for more
time? One must be possessed by the spirit of play even to
imagine the possibility. Yet probably every human being has
had experiences of powerful and significant time. A moment
of relationship with another, a moment of insight into meaning, a moment of visual perception, a moment of physical
movement—such times have occurred in which conflict,
bondage, and anxiety over yesterday, today, tomorrow, and
eternity were impossible. They were moments of adventure.

The nature of myth is also illuminated by the human responses to it related to the term "believing." It is easy for
the adult to respond to a child's story or an adult novel in
terms of make-believing and still value it. But it has not
been so easy for him to be possessed by the same approach
to the bigger tales we call myths. Yet what is appropriate

for the little story is appropriate for the big story. It follows
from the theory of play and religion already outlined that
the secular response to myth is that of *disbelieving,* the
magical response is that of *believing,* and the religious response is that of *make-believing.* Analysis of the rationale
of these responses will give further insight into the nature
of religion as play.

The secular response to the mythical story is disbelieving.
Disbelieving is acknowledgment that the profane man cannot get what he desires from the sacred story. This can
occur in at least two circumstances. First, the individual
may actually hear the story being told as "just" a story. In
such an event, no promises are given, no claims made, and
no hopes aroused. The worker hears nothing that will assist
him in overcoming the conflicts of his struggling life. Moreover, since the sacred appears threatening to the profane
world, he may conclude that the myth not only fails to aid
his struggles but even interrupts and destroys them. There
is no choice but to disbelieve as emphatically as possible.
Just hearing the "old, old story" has no appeal and is considered a waste of time, or it threatens the hearer by its
revelation of something different. Second, the secular person
may hear more about dogma and creeds than about the story
itself. This, indeed, is far more likely for contemporary man,
as sacred stories are no longer told in any straightforward
fashion. On the one hand, he may practice believing in them
to attain what he desires (survival, and all that assists this
goal), and fail. So he disbelieves because the story does not
work for his profane ends. On the other hand, he may *correctly* realize that dogmas and creeds really have nothing to
do with the profane world and respond by ignoring them. In
any case, the worker discovers that the sacred story is quite
unrelated to his present life and so disbelieves.

The magical response to myth is believing. Whereas disbelieving is the conviction that myth will not assist the

worker, believing is acknowledgment that the worker can
receive what he desires. The magician becomes quite concerned about the validity of the story and so believes. The
magical mingling of the sacred and the profane issues in the
promotion of believing. Believing is acknowledgment of the
sacred for the sake of the profane, a work reaction to the
manifestation of new energy and new design in the story.
One always believes "because." The mother believes in play
because it will remove her child's restlessness. The adult believes in the sacred because he will receive wealth or health
(survival). The statement "I believe" is always incomplete.
So the primitive magician affirms, "If I pronounce the sacred
words over the sacred symbol, I will catch my fish," and the
modern magician states, "If I say my prayers, I will receive
strength for tomorrow." Consequently, the call to believe is
usually accompanied by promise of benefit or threat of harm,
and these promises refer to the struggles of profane living.
Even such seemingly benign statements as "I believe because
of what God has done for me" or " I believe because I have
received meaning for my life" represent the attempt to make
the sacred useful for profane life. This attitude is quite apparent in children who pray for something and then believe
or disbelieve according to the results. And there is little
reason to assume that all human beings grow up in this respect. The magician is a pragmatist who believes the sacred
story is true because it works. Thus, believing is the result
of an inappropriate work response to what offers the potentiality for play. Myth is purposeless, and the attempt to
use it is antireligious.

It seems likely that a majority of people live in between
the two poles of disbelief and belief, shuffling back and
forth between disappointment and hope. Disbelief may control in most situations, but belief gains ascendancy in times
of crisis. The foxholes of life are filled by magicians. Man's
ability to compartmentalize prevents both confusion and

insight, so the conflict between disbelief and belief reigns. Perhaps this reign is facilitated by the fact that conventional piety assimilates both poles with equal facility.

In the religious response to the sacred story, the conflict between believing and disbelieving is transcended by make-believing. The religious response to the sacred is complete acceptance, a primal recognition that something has happened. As stated previously in the discussion of the element of freedom, the sacred is autonomous. In the religious response, the myth is acknowledged as autonomous. The story is neither doubted nor buttressed by belief, because it is there. To use Eliade's term, the story is "true" simply because it exists. To judge is to stand outside the story in the profane world, and this is precisely what the religious person cannot do. Perhaps even the term "make-believing" is inadequate and reflects the point of view of the outsider. The player is not making-believe or deliberately making anything. If a hungry man sees an apple, he picks it up and eats it. If he first doubts the correctness of his eyesight or pauses to wonder if the apple would be in existence if he were out of its presence, his sanity is precarious (unless he is a philosopher, perhaps). The player on any level is no different. The inherently natural reaction to a story is to tell it in actions and words. And for the one who fully participates in the story, *nothing else is required.* Questions of truth and falsity remain irrelevant, indeed, even incomprehensible. Unless believing and disbelieving are transcended, the life of adventure in the partial play of the immature, or in the full play of the religious adult, does not occur.

It follows from what has been said that the most likely *religious* addition to a myth is another story. This has been the traditional approach, namely, the gathering of a group of stories all related to a central one. The little stories pertaining to an individual's or society's life are taken up and given additional meaning by the big story. However, myths have also been surrounded with dogmas, creeds, and theologies. Magic being rather persistent in man, it is probable that these accretions are mostly the result of profane responses to the sacred. Perversions of religious play are most common, and that perversion of preservation which most frequently occurs in apologetic theology may head the list. Yet this is not inevitable. Since any human activity may be playful, dogmatizing and theologizing cannot be excluded from this possibility. If such activity is regarded as unnecessary, useless, far from definitive, and as only a gracious offering of the mind for the sake of full play, it is appropriately playful and allows the sacred story to remain uncorrupted and autonomous.

The conclusion is that the secular response to myth is disbelieving, the magical response is believing, and that the religious response is make-believing. Thus, there is a similarity between the religious and the secular responses, for it is only the magician who believes that myth will work in the profane world. The distinction between the two is that one reacts negatively, and the other positively. The magical person tries to make myth effective in daily life, the secular person unhappily accepts this as impossible, and the religious person rejoices in myth for its own sake.

Modern adults are accustomed to leave pretending and make-believing to children. But primitive man is like the child in this respect. An anthropologist writes:

> Just as the savage is a good actor, throwing himself like a child into his mime, so he is a good spectator, entering into the spirit of another's acting, herein again resembling the child, who can be frightened into fits by the roar of what he knows to be but a "pretended" lion.[16]

The child, the primitive, and the saint are all alike. In his discussion of religion as make-believing, Huizinga refers to St. Francis' devotion to his bride, Poverty. Noting that

Francis was completely devoted, he asks if it can really be said that he believed in a spiritual being by that name, and concludes that neither the Church nor St. Francis could have simply answered positively:

> St. Francis' attitude was one of belief and unbelief mixed. The Church hardly authorized him in an explicit belief of that sort. His conception of Poverty must have vacillated between poetic imagination and dogmatic conviction, although gravitating toward the latter. The most succinct way of putting his state of mind would be to say that St. Francis was playing with the figure of poverty.[17]

The religious saint delights in the humor and exaggeration of divine tales. The difference between a tall tale of Baron Munchausen and those tallest of tall tales which are sacred stories is only one of degree, and the appropriate response to both is identical. A story cannot be participated in and manipulated at the same time. It can either be enjoyed or used, but not both. What would it be like to stop disbelieving, or to stop believing, or, indeed, to stop both? As a mature player, one would relate to the ancient sacred stories, even the story of the Word become flesh, just as he participates in the most contemporary poem, novel, drama, or joke —with peace, freedom, delight, and illusion. How else could an individual participate in those gigantic absurdities and enormous exaggerations which abound in all holy hyperbole? How else could one be grasped by the Christian story—the tallest tale ever told? How else could one dance before the Ark?

Ritual.   It cannot be overemphasized that myth and ritual are only aspects of what is basically a single response to the sacred. And it follows that ritual is as much a way of life as it is a special action at a special time, just as the story is a way of living. For the adventurer, the festival highlights what exists more subtly at other times. Thus, ritual is a way of life that is exposed and renewed by specific ritual events. Such events among primitive man as knocking out a human tooth, frenzied dancing, and sacrifice of animals seem so distant and bizarre to modern man as to require analysis for the sake of understanding more contemporary ritual. The discussion of ritual begins with an understanding provided by the historians of religion and is followed by an interpretation with emphasis on the place of space and sacrifice.

The first thing students of religion point out is that religion requires, not just passive acceptance of the sacred, but active attitudes as well. Lessa and Vogt state the general conclusion that religion consists of both beliefs *and* practices.[18] The beliefs are expressed in myths and the practices are prescribed in rituals. Rituals are those procedures, such as worshiping, praying, chanting, sacrificing, and making offerings, that are carried out in response to the sacred. Ritual acts are things to be done with regard to the manifestation of the holy. As Van der Leeuw suggests, the sacred reveals possibility and this demands activity: man's experience of the sacred power must "expand into *conduct* and his conduct, still further, into celebration. . . ."[19] On the smallest scale this would include such gestures as standing, prostrating, and kneeling. Since sacred power is typically manifest on the occasions of birth, initiation, marriage, sickness, journeys, war, and death, it is these times of crisis which most clearly produce the celebrative life of ritual. But to state that ritual is practice related to the most important concerns of man reveals no more than the statement that myth is belief, and can be just as misleading. Understanding of religious action in ritual requires attention to two things —space and dance. There can be no action without orientation in space, and full orientation in space leads to the action of dance.

Eliade observes that as the sacred interrupts time, so also

does it break into profane space. Primitive man assumes a strong difference and opposition between the land he inhabits and the space that surrounds it. The former is cosmos and the latter is chaos. Chaotic space is "homogeneous and neutral" with no qualitative differences in the parts of the mass.[20] It represents the chaos which ruled before the sacred founded the world and which may return when the power of the sacred diminishes. To the contrary, sacred space is ordered. Eliade writes:

> For it is the break effected in space that allows the world to be constituted, because it reveals the fixed points, the central axis for all future orientation. . . . The manifestation of the sacred ontologically founds the world. In the homogeneous and infinite expanse, in which no point of reference is possible and hence no orientation can be established, the hierophany reveals an absolute fixed point, a center.[21]

It follows that if a place is to be lived in, that is, acted in, the place must be *founded*. If no sacred sign occurs, one is asked for. The Vedic ritual for taking possession of new land reveals this necessity. Possession occurs by building a fire altar to Agni. The water used represents the primordial waters, the clay symbolizes the earth, and the walls of the latter suggest the sky. The creation of the altar requires songs that claim the cosmic regions are being created. What all this means is that taking possession of the new land is a repetition of the original creation of the world. What is unknown and chaotic becomes known and cosmic by repeating the original acts of the gods. The identical dynamic is found in all acts of consecration. The house, temple, or city must be certified by a sacred sign or properly consecrated. The necessary ritual is always a repetition of the original work of the gods.

But what occurs in the original, and in all subsequent

foundings of the world, is more than just the creation of a fixed point in the midst of chaos. The fixed point is more than a geometric symbol. Every sacred space is the very center of the world, being a break in profane space, an opening to the sacred, and a means of communication between the sacred and the profane. The New England village green and the Maypole are remnants of a primitive awareness of the importance of the center of existence. What is most important to man is the location of the "navel of the earth." Among the primitives, a sacred pole commonly represents this center where earth, the underworld, and the heavens are put into communication. The fixed point provides not only orientation on earth but also between earth and the other realms. And the primitive believes that he must live as close as possible to this center for the sake of orientation. It is only the gods who provide orientation for action. As Eliade puts it, "the world becomes apprehensible as world, as cosmos, in the measure in which it reveals itself as a sacred world."[22] To exist only in the chaos of profane space would be to succumb to anxiety and be shocked into inaction. If, as frequently happens, a cosmic pillar or other symbol of the center is destroyed, a whole village becomes inactive, awaits its death, and the members do physically die often enough. Without sacred orientation, there is no possibility of that action which is life. The need of man is to live as it was in the beginning, when the cosmos came fresh from the Creator.

Van der Leeuw has written: "When something matters in life, one feels festive; the expression of life becomes stylized into a fixed, rhythmical form."[23] The statement offers a useful definition of ritual. The sacred is what matters, and when it is manifest to man, the response is the festive rhythm that is sacred ritual. For primitive peoples, religion and the arts were inseparable if not identical. And the simplest, oldest, and most powerful of all the arts is beautiful motion. Van der Leeuw poetically defines dance in a manner that would be fully appreciated by primitive man:

> The dance is indeed the movement of man in the literal sense, but it is not his natural movement, being rather the specifically human movement created by him. It is ordered movement. The dance is a movement of the self in a purposeful, definite manner. It is walking the way we walked as children, with one foot on the sidewalk and the other in the street; or three steps forward on the right foot, then one on the left. In the dance, man discovers the rhythm of the motion that surrounds him, just as it surrounds another man or an animal or a star. He discovers the rhythm and invents a response, but it is a response that has its own forms, that is stylized and ordered. He does with motion that same thing that he does with a shape when he carves or chisels, draws or paints. He places his own movements and those of the creatures which surround him into an ordered whole.[24]

The point being made is that the sacred founds the cosmos by providing orientation and that this orientation is essentially rhythm. The sacred is manifest as rhythm, and the religious response is the dance. Dance is the source of the other arts—music, song, drama. Ritual embodies all the arts, but it is fundamentally dance. The sacred grants full action, and full action is dancing.

Van der Leeuw considers the intimacy of religion and dance with respect to pantomime, ecstasy, and the movement of God. The dance pantomime clearly reveals that, contrary to modern man, the primitive danced on the occasions that were the *most* significant for him. The hunting dances, fertility dances, love dances, and war dances focus on the basic concerns of life. The primitive cannot live without them: "My dancing, drinking and singing weave me the mat on which my soul will sleep in the world of the spirits."[25]

For in dancing, the participants become actors who hunt, love, and kill according to the occasion. They wear a phallus or a mask and become animals or even the gods. That the dancers take their action seriously is indicated by the fact that Mexican Indians have a single word both for dancing and working. And the most primitive and universal occurrence of dance in pantomime form clearly demonstrates the fundamental connection between ritual and myth. The primitive way to tell a story is to dance it out.

Van der Leeuw believes that all dance is ecstatic to some degree. One becomes possessed by the dance and does not dance, but "is danced."

> Thus the rhythm of the dance reaches out and conquers the world. But contemporaneously with the outreaching movement and constantly alternating with it, there unfolds the contrary movement which discards life. The dance, by its very nature, is ecstatic. It makes man beside himself, lifts him above life and the world, and lets his whole earthly existence perish in the maelstrom.[26]

This intoxication is apparent in the frenzy of the Sufi dancers who spin themselves out of normal consciousness and in the more primitive Kwakiuti Indians of North America who eat human flesh in a state of terror and disgust. Sacred dance throws the participant into another world.

That dance deals with what is significant in this world by participation in another world means that dance is basically cosmic. The dance that man knows is a result of the primal dance initiated by the gods. In the beginning was not the word, but the dance, or, better, the word was dance. What the primitive knew intuitively, was rediscovered by the mystics. According to the Hindus, the dance of Shiva is the source of all movement in the cosmos, both sustains and destroys all existence, and occurs within the heart of man. And the Christian mystics have dwelt on the metaphor of

the dance. Van der Leeuw quotes a product of Bernardine
mysticism:

> Jesus the dancers' master is,
> A great skill at the dance is his,
> He turns to right, he turns to left;
> All must follow his teaching deft.[27]

What was true of the heavens at the time of creation and
true of the angels even now, is to become true of the dis-
ciple of Christ—all must dance to the tune of the Lord.

A way to put some flesh on the abstract bones of these
conclusions is to consider a specific ritual of the Papago
Indians of the Southwest desert.[28] To be an agricultural people in the midst of arid land is to be concerned about fertility and rain. The fertility rite occurred when the first few
drops of rain commenced in the early summer. A sacred
liquor was prepared from cactus buds which became the
focus of the ritual. For two nights the whole village would
sing and dance. In a clear space before the council house
the people sat. Swirling his rattle four times, the leader
began the rain song of the village:

> At the edge of the mountain
> A cloud hangs.
> And there my heart, my heart, my heart,
> Hangs with it.

The leader would begin to circle the small fire in the center
of the clear space, and the men would join him, holding
hands and moving slowly clockwise.

> At the edge of the mountain
> The cloud trembles.
> And there my heart, my heart, my heart,
> Trembles with it.

Then the women would move into the space, separate the
men's hands, take partners, and continue the circling dance

with them. All would dance the whole night with occasional inspection of the brewing liquor. At dawn, the medicine man would announce: "Go home now. Sleep. Tomorrow we shall dance again, that the corn may grow, the beans may grow, the squash may grow."

The ritual of the Papago is about rain and fertility. It is a celebration of the appearance of the buds of cacti and drops of rain. As a celebration is an action, not the passive participation of spectators, but the active dance of all concerned, is provoked. The clear space for dance is sacred space, that center of the universe which brings order out of chaos and establishes a flow of communication with the sacred. What occurs is what occurred in the beginning—the founding of the world. And the response of the Indians is that dance which is pantomime, ecstasy, and also the movement of the gods themselves. What would it be like to live as a primitive person in an area in which rain falls only one third of the year, to see the buds develop and the drops fall, and then to participate in the ritual? It would be to be possessed by the rhythm that creates and sustains existence and makes it a joy forever. It would be to possess power and orientation for life in this world. It would be these things because it would be to exist in the sacred space which had all the purity and freshness of space when it was first created by the holy. It would be to dance out one's life and to be danced out by life. It would be to act fully. So, to live in the sacred place of the ritual is really to live.

The general perspective added by the theory of this essay to the conclusions of the historians of religion should be apparent. The full adventure that is lived and communicated as ritual as well as myth is a result of the harmony of the needs of discharge of energy and design of experience. As asserted previously, sacred space is play space and the arena for the sacred is the playground. A playground is oriented ground. To participate in it is to discover where one is and where one can go. Full action, that which is ritual, occurs only when this founding exists, for such action can result only when objects are perceived in relationship. And the extremes of chaotic movement and paralysis are replaced by the full movement of dance. To receive grace from the sacred is to be made graceful. This identity of play and dance is fully acknowledged by Huizinga:

> Whether we think of the sacred or magical dances of savages, or of the Greek ritual dances, or of the dancing of King David before the Ark of the Covenant, or of the dance simply as part of a festival, it is always at all periods and with all peoples pure play, the purest and most perfect form of play that exists. . . . It is not that dancing has something of play in it or about it, rather that it is an integral part of play: the relationship is one of direct participation, almost of essential identity. Dancing is a particular and particularly perfect form of playing.[29]

Needless to say, such dance is not merely of the body, but of the total personality in full play when the sacred calls the tune. Thus ritual is an adventuresome participation in space which is characterized by the gift of graceful movement.

Where does such space occur for contemporary man? Since an adventure is a surprise, it could occur anywhere. A few individuals may find no space, and they live in perpetual awkwardness and constant fear of mishap. For another few, it may exist in the sacred ground and ritual of the traditional church. Their worship may so orient and found them that they are able to dance out into all of their life space. But perhaps most individuals find a less powerful and less organized space that still allows some dancing—the little spaces of the sports field, theater, house, and office. Ritual exists in such spaces, however immature it may be. And a little dance is better than none.

But ritual is also a game—a game for the fully mature who

experience the sacred. As a playtime is for stories, so a playground is for games. Whether it be a hopscotch diagram, card table, tennis court, or sports arena, common play requires a specific space and all other space is out of bounds. And within this space, there are rules for play. As stated previously, there is no such thing as "free-play" in the psychological sense, but always rules for playing the game. Since rules occur in the secular and magical responses to the sacred as well as in the religious response, some analysis of the differences are appropriate.

The habit of primitive man in carrying out his ritual actions in a very precise way is commented upon by all anthropologists. An example of this meticulousness is a ritual of the Tikopia which involved the plaiting of mats used in the temples.[30] The women came from several groups and had to be seated in a definite order. Their backs had to be to the sea. A taboo of silence was imposed. The space in which they "worked" was sacred and they could not be approached by anyone else. Even the place from which raw material was gathered for the plaiting could not be used for ordinary work. This part of the ritual was very minor, but careful attention to detailed rules was important. From the view of a secular worker, many unnecessary hardships were accepted. But what was at stake was not the profane, but the sacred.

It is possible that for some of the women the ritual could have been no more than the boring routine of secular living. In this case, the rules grew out of profane routine and were obeyed for the sake of the profane. Secular rules exist for the preservation of routine, that desperate strategy of organizing chaos for the sake of survival. And it follows that such rules are enforced compulsively by the profane worker. For chaos may break in at any moment due to the pressure of the need for discharge of energy. Compulsive attachment to rules is an indication of the fear of forthcoming chaos.

But it is also possible that the rules followed by these

primitive women developed out of that complicated response to the sacred known as magic. In this case, the rules grew out of both profane routine and sacred rhythm. As depicted previously, such a magical response is more characterized by fear than anything else. Thus, the magician is even more compulsive than the worker. The female magician in this case would fear both the breakdown of the profane into chaos and the presumed "chaos" brought by the sacred. So, if the woman participated in the plaiting of mats in an attempt to use sacred power for profane ends, she would hold to the rules all the more compulsively for fear of destruction. Thus, it is because of the secular and magical responses to the sacred that "religious" rituals foster scrupulosity.

But rules do not need to be held to compulsively. The rules of the game of plaiting are necessary accompaniments, but not crucial in and of themselves. The awareness behind the concept of the spirit over the law was perfectly realized by primitive man. The rules about plaiting indicate the significance of the "work," the turning of the backs to the sea, for example, indicating their respect for the sacred area on the farther shore. But this does not mean that the rules force the sacred to appear and grant man's desires. A game is a contest, requiring skill or luck or both. This means that it may not necessarily come off to the player's satisfaction. No game, even the ritual game, is sure-fire. Sacred ritual is never effective automatically as the magician would like to believe, but depends on the spirit of both man and the gods to make it a holy adventure. This fact is acknowledged by the player. The religious participant in ritual follows all the rules, but is not dependent on them. He follows the rules because he enjoys them as the sacred designs that illuminate his life. His repetition is a delight rather than a defense, a sign of respect rather than coercion. If the game does not come off to his satisfaction, he is amazed and amused rather than defeated and destroyed. All this is to say that whereas the rules of the profane proceed from routine and the rules of the magician proceed against sacred rhythm, the rules of the religious person proceed *from* rhythm. What is important is the rhythm, not the rules. It is only the sacred rhythm which creates them and gives them meaning.

The reader might observe others, or himself, in any contemporary ritual. Participation in Holy Communion or New Year's Eve festivities could occur for the secular reasons of maintaining social and business contacts. Or the rituals could be followed magically for the sake of gaining better health, more money, or stronger relations with another person. Now and then, it might be possible to glimpse in another or oneself, participation for the sake of the ritual itself. Only in the latter case would the observance proceed from rhythm. The secular individual can be likened to one who only sees a piece of sheet music and does not participate by playing the tune. The magician attempts to play, but is out of tune and misses the beat. The religious person sees the sheet of music, is caught up by the beat, and plays the tune. Further, the music becomes second nature to him, so he does not have to refer to the sheet so often and, indeed, may even improvise. The rules remain, but fully serve rhythm. Only for the religious individual is the game of ritual really played.

The nature of ritual is illuminated also by the human responses to it which involve "sacrifice." The common usage of this term varies considerably from traditional and primitive usage. The contemporary meaning signifies a kind of secular renunciation that is a hardship and may or may not "pay off" for the individual. In his work, *Sacrifice in Greek and Roman Religions and Early Judaism*, Royden Keith Yerkes schematizes the difference between the modern popular meaning and the more traditional religious meaning in the following way:[31]

	ANCIENT	MODERN
Field of use	Wholly religious. Never used secularly.	Almost wholly secular; transfered to religious use.
Purpose	Solely a cultic act.	Never a cultic act.
Size of sacrifice	As large as possible.	As small as possible.
Recipient	Always offered *to* a god, thus indicating a recognition of superiority.	Never offered *to* anyone.
Performance and accompanying emotions	Always performed with joy; came to be identified with thanksgiving.	Always performed with regret; accompanied by sadness.
Significant emphasis	Emphasis on giving and action. Deprivation, while a necessary fact as with all giving, never a constituent factor of the sacrifice.	Emphasis always on giving *up* and on deprivation.
Death of the thing sacrificed	Wholly incidental and never with any inherent or significant meaning. A fact but never a factor in the sacrifice.	Signifies the "supreme sacrifice." A necessary factor in all sacrifice.

This brief analysis of the distinction between two uses of the term indicates some need for more careful examination of the nature of ritual, for all ritual is sacrifice. The basic theory of this essay is that the secular response is that of *suffering without sacrifice,* the magical response that of *sacrifice with suffering,* and the religious response that of *sacrifice without suffering.*

The secular response to sacred ritual is that signified by Yerkes under the category of "modern." His list of characteristics of this view of sacrifice correctly indicates the dynamics of the secular, but not necessarily modern, individual. The person who lives in conflict is constantly giving up to the demands of the two basic needs. He suffers and does not consider himself to be in a position to increase his suffering. His view of the sacred ritual is such that it appears to require this increase. The common sayings of the magicians who inform their society may reinforce this reaction. Or, as in the case of myth, the secular person may realize that the magician is mistaken and that the promised benefits will not be received, or that they are illusory. The worker cannot anticipate harmony and can only continue to struggle with, and suffer over, his problems. Whether sacrifice be interpreted traditionally or magically, he cannot perform it and must live with his meaningless suffering.

The magical response to sacrifice frequently is the *implicit* theme in the discussion of ritual by Caillois. He understands the primitive as believing the sacred to be the source of all good luck and success. Collective ecstasy in the festive is a witness in advance to the promise of fertile women, brave warriors, and good fishing. It is not surprising that his theory of the sacrifice by primitive man is equally magical:

> Yet the supplicant can imagine nothing better, in order to control the Gods and have them yield to him, than to take the initiative by making them a gift or a *sacrifice,* that is by consecrating, by presenting at his expense to the domain of the sacred, something that belongs to him and that he gives up, something of which he has free disposition and to which he renounces every right.[32]

According to Caillois, all sacrificial practices and the practice of the sacrificial life of asceticism follow the principle of

Thus, it can be concluded that there is a similarity between the magical and secular responses, for both acknowledge suffering as a part of sacrifice. The distinction between the two is that the one reacts positively and the other negatively. The secular person rejects sacrificial suffering as unbearable and futile, the magical person accepts such suffering for future gain, and the religious person does not suffer.

The player's assertion, "Be not anxious," appears foolish and callous to the worker. Indeed, contemporary man seems to hallow suffering and proclaim, "Be anxious." The jibe of foolishness occurs because the worker experiences no alternative to anxiety and concludes, "If I can't lick it, I'll join it." Suffering is given more than its due. The jibe of callousness occurs because the worker may well suspect that his concern for others is based on his own suffering. He suggests that one who did not suffer inwardly would not be concerned about others. As noted previously, it is the player who, in being free from psychic suffering, is free to perceive and enter into the suffering of others. It is the worker who is foolish and callous. This issue is complicated by the kind of attention it has received from the "religious" traditions. It is often assumed that the suffering of God in heaven and God in Christ is identical in quality to the suffering of man the sinner. But Jesus was going about his father's business, not his own. To suffer over oneself and suffer over others are two quite different things. Anyone who has recovered from a case of neurotic anxiety knows the difference. Since most people suffer over themselves most of the time, perhaps another term should be used to indicate the "suffering" of God and his occasional adventurers. The mature player sacrifices with peace, freedom, illusion, and delight.

Our purpose has been to fill out the basic theory of religion as play by consideration of myth and ritual. All that has been affirmed about stories and games for children applies to those stories and games for mature adults that are called myths and rituals. The sacred is manifest to man as power, and man responds secularly, magically, or religiously. Since the sacred is always powerful form, these three responses occur in the stories that are told and the games that are acted. The two modes are one in the meaningful and graceful action of adventure. If the reader has begun to perceive that the magical response is more common than any other and that the secular response is more common than the religious, his perception is identical to that of the author. High adventure, at any level of maturity, is a rare and surprising event. The gift of a new self with a new time and a new space that is beyond belief and suffering, is no commonplace occurrence. Rather, it is, as correctly perceived by religious man, a miracle.

6 In Praise of Play ....

WHEN a group of distinguished news commentators was asked, "What is the gravest crisis facing the American people in the years ahead?" most of the replies focused on international affairs. But when it came Eric Sevareid's turn to speak, he stated that the most dangerous threat to our country was the rise of leisure.[1] Part of the problem and its source is indicated by the comment of a psychiatrist, Franz Alexander:

> It is paradoxical that when man through scientific knowledge has become too efficient in securing with little effort the basic necessities of life, he becomes so deadly serious and looks nostalgically at the creative centuries of the past during which he still had the time and the detachment necessary for play and creativity. In this paradox lies the secret of understanding the crisis of Western civilization.[2]

Accordingly, our purpose has not been to provide any new and novel approach to the problem of leisure, but to recall a very ancient and traditional point of view. Nostalgia has lead the author back to primitive man who had to work hard to survive, but also had time and space for play. This temporary retreat from contemporary culture and religion has an advantage well stated by the orientalist, Heinrich Zimmer:

> . . . the real treasure, that which can put an end to our poverty and all our trials, is never very far; there is no need to seek it in a distant country. It lies buried in the most intimate parts of our own house; that is, of our own being. . . . And yet—there is this strange and persistent fact, that it is only after a pious journey in a distant region, in a new land, that the meaning of that inner voice guiding us on our search can make itself understood by us.[3]

Such a retreat is only temporary, but it may be necessary because of the amalgamation of current "religion" with contemporary work culture.

A full return from retreat is beyond the scope of this essay and is a challenge for the reader. Everyone has had the required experience. Although most of us work most of the time and play pervertedly and immaturely, everyone has tasted of the spirit of play. Some adults have had this experience encompass their total being to such an extent that the holy has been acknowledged by a religious response. If this has not happened to an adult, then a sense of what can be and should be is available, provided he is capable of recalling the past adventures of immaturity. Everyone knows what it would be like to participate in the story and game of the adventure of God in Christ. Everyone knows what it would be like to partake of Holy Communion, to kneel, sing, taste, and become a child of God in God's world with the spirit of peace, freedom, delight, and unworldliness. Consider the play of the child, and the nature of the Kingdom will be revealed. Christ is that fiddler who plays so sweetly that all who hear him begin to dance. But those who prefer to be deaf and know nothing of music will perceive him as a madman and view the dancers as senseless and in bad taste.

What has been written is an elaboration of an impression

about life that does not aim toward absolute truth. In the
field of sports, a "dead" ball is a ball that is out of play. To
be "dead right" or "dead certain" means just what is said—
to be dead. To be alive is to be uncertain and doubtful. But
these are the negative terms of the worker who desires that
absolute arrival which is death. The word for the player is
surprise. This theory of play has been presented because the
author has been surprised a few times and places and hopes
that the readers will savor their surprises. The Holy might
well be defined as the Surprising, and joyfully to anticipate
and savor the Surprising is the playful response of the religious man. What could be more surprising than the story of
the Word become flesh and the game of Communion which
celebrates it? So, this theory of play is part of an adventure,
and future surprises may drastically change the impressions
about life that have been given.

Since no new surprise has occurred at this moment, a
conclusion is in order that states the fundamental theme in
different ways that are appropriate to problems of modern
man. One way is to speak of death. This final event in life
which is so avoided by modern man is a crucial aspect of
life for the player and religious man. The other way is to
consider the desperate need of the contemporary church to
be relevant to the world and reverent to God. Sufficient
clues have been given to indicate that the spirit of play
creates irrelevance to the world and irreverence to God.

Death and Rebirth.   It has been asserted repeatedly that
the adventurer is not concerned about success and survival.
But he is concerned about a new life and new world. The
stories that are told and the games that are played in a fully
religious adventure concern death and rebirth. To grasp the
nature of this concern, it is useful to examine first the attitude of modern man toward death.

The approach of modern man to death is epitomized by
the statement a man once made to his wife: "If one of us

dies, I'll go to Paris." For a human creature, to be alive is to know consciously that one has to die. Some have made the most of this consciousness, Maeterlinck proclaiming: "There is only one event, in our life and in our universe, that really counts, and this is death." But the vast majority of contemporary men do not use this consciousness of death. Indeed, it does its best to become unconscious of death. Denial of death is an art at which we excel, and there are as many ways to go about it as there are human beings, but three obvious methods can be noted.

The first method is simply to ignore death in toto. A classic example was the traditional policy of the *Christian Science Monitor* that did not permit use of the term "death." The modern life insurance salesman does not ask, "How will your family be taken care of if you should die tomorrow?" Rather, he is instructed to say, "How would your family be taken care of if you had died yesterday?" The former question gives rise to fears that do not assist the salesman, but the latter states a comfortable impossibility. Our first reaction to death is totally to ignore it if at all possible.

In the second method, we do not totally ignore death but deny its harshness. It is somewhat dazzling to behold modern man's inventiveness in this respect. Harshness is denied by all the euphemisms used. We do not die nowadays, we "expire," "depart," "pass away," or "pass on"; sometimes, we just "sleep." We do not fill in a death certificate, but complete a "vital statistics form." We attempt to preserve and prettify the corpse, trying to create the illusion of life, or, at least, momentary sleep; and we customarily observe to the bereaved that this painted corpse looks "very natural." The language and action revealed at the occasion of death illustrate a need to deny the harshness of death.

The third common method of denying death is more subtle and may even seem to refute the claim that contemporary man strives to deny. In one way, modern society seems preoccupied with death. Some newspapers maintain a large circulation by vivid portrayal of violent death. The comic books, westerns, detective stories, and spy novels achieve mass communication by inclusion of numerous and detailed presentations of violent death. But this contemporary fascination with death is also a form of denial, for the social anthropologist, Geoffrey Gorer, has shown it to be pornographic.[4]

Pornography has always been associated with sex. It refers to material created in order to excite man sexually. This material and our response to it lack all the feelings that make man human. A breast or penis is presented as an object. Even a whole body is not presented or responded to as a person. The private fantasies can be nothing but that of doing something to an object, each fantasy becoming more complicated and sensational than the last. Sexual pornography is a way of fulfilling a sexual need without being involved with another person. It is a way of denying the personal aspects of sex. This occurs most frequently when a society is prudish. When sex is considered disgusting or immoral and not to be talked about and participated in, sexual need is not destroyed but only forced into inhuman paths. And, of course, pornography may occur in any individual who lacks sufficient trust to relate to another human being.

The pornography of death follows the same dynamic. The mass media make little bid for our normal feelings of sorrow and love at the occasion of death. The creators of Mike Hammer and James Bond seemed only to be making each successive novel contain more spectacular ways of dying. And our typical response contains no more genuine human feeling than that of the collector of filthy pictures. If modern man seeks out death, it is only to deny it. He may not deny death in toto or deny its harshness, but actually emphasize the harshness in order to deny the personal aspect of death.

This occurs partially because this society is prudish about death, sees death as disgusting and immoral and not to be talked about. Yet, since there is a fundamental need to come to terms with all elements of life, including dying and death, the end result is pornographic perversion. And man also may be ruled by this perversion insofar as he lacks sufficient trust to relate to life.

These three examples of how modern man works to flee the fact of death indicate an awareness quite different from that of the religious man. For contrast, it is appropriate to move entirely out of contemporary American culture into the life of a ten-year-old boy who lives in the primitive village of Australian Bushmen. He is about to pass through the puberty rite of initiation into manhood. The ritual has two stages—death and rebirth.

After the older men have prepared a sacred place in the bush, the mother brings her son to the edge of the village. She does not know the content of the rites. She has heard only rumors about death and manhood. She does know that occasionally a child fails to return. The little boy knows the same. Both are filled with excitement and pride, but also with great anxiety. The men rush forward and force the boy away from his mother. She weeps and wails over the forthcoming death of her son. He is taken to a hut where he lies down on his back and with his arms crossed over his chest. He is covered with a rug and told not to utter a sound. During the coming days, he may be symbolically burned by a fire, buried in a shallow pit, be ritually dismembered, or have a tooth knocked out. All these things—the separation from his mother, the darkness, and the physical dangers—are symbolic experiences of death. The boy is told that the gods are killing him. He does not know for sure whether he will literally survive or not. By means of this first half of the puberty ritual, the world of the child and his personality are destroyed.

The second half of the ritual takes place over an extended period of time. The boy meets his god and receives his name. After this he may have to be fed by a guardian for as much as six months, for newborn infants cannot feed themselves without help. During this time he is instructed and trained to meditate on his experiences. By story, dance, and pantomime, he is introduced to the gods, the history of the tribe, and to the way he is to live. Finally, the boy is returned to the community to take his place as a new person in a new world. The boy and his mother may not acknowledge each other for some time to come. After all, her son has died, it is a strange adult who returned to the village. In the spiritual sense, the boy does not know his mother. His old world and old self have been destroyed. Death has led to rebirth and to a new creation.

These examples of contemporary and primitive responses to death demonstrate that the former flees death and that the latter seeks death. The examples may overstate the case, but the difference is considerable nevertheless. It is possible that this difference may be due to the fact that the understanding of primitive man is, in the phrases of Eliade, "that a state cannot be changed without first being annihilated," and that "access to spiritual life always entails death to the profane condition, followed by a new birth."[5] To be specific, contrary to some modern interpretations of the ritual, the puberty rite was not considered to be only a tool for growing up and passing through the stage of adolescence quickly and with little difficulty. To lie down in a grave is not the same as to recline on an analyst's couch. The puberty ritual existed to create a human being. Before the rite took place, the boy was not a human being at all; he was only an animal who might become a human being someday. By means of the rite, he was brought in touch with the powerful form of the sacred which transformed him. This is to say that the boy was moved from a profane condition to a sacred one.

What is profane is not real, and it is not human. The sacred is not a tool for growing up, but a gift of humanity. And the gift must be preceded by death.

The religious man, in whatever age and culture, is the one who acknowledges that the sacred requires death to the profane and joyfully accepts this condition. The magical man does not accept this understanding, but attempts a partial death in order to achieve, not a new birth, but a strengthening of the profane. The secular individual simply refuses to die. All these responses may indicate awareness of the decaying world, but the secular man seeks only to check or slow the rate of decay; the magical man attempts to reverse the process of decay into one of growth; the religious man leaves the decay of this world for the new world of the sacred and returns to find the old world renewed. Whereas the secular man remains in the condition of work and the magical man remains in the condition of the perversion of play, the religious man enters into a new life of adventure. What modern man tends to forget is that there is no rebirth which is not preceded by death.

Our conclusion is that the profane world of inner conflict is the world that leads to death and that the sacred world of inner harmony is the world that leads to life. The basic situation of man is filled with irony: those most concerned about survival participate in a kind of living death, while those not concerned about survival participate in a new life. This reflects the understanding of primitive man and the awareness of any mature adventurer in any age. The destruction of the chaotic and weary world of conflict is the death of death. Entrance into the orderly and potent world of harmony is the birth of life.

Concerning the longing of primitive man for the sacred, Eliade writes:

> Let me point out that this desire is no "spiritual" attitude, which depreciates life on earth and all that goes with it in

favour of a "spirituality" of detachment from the world. On
the contrary, what may be called the "nostalgia for eternity"
proves that man longs for a concrete paradise, and believes
that such a paradise can be won *here,* on earth, and *now,*
in the present moment.[6]

It is the worker who anticipates a "somewhere" and "some-
time" and then becomes disillusioned about a "never-never
land." Dogmas and doctrines of eternal life are a snare and a
delusion if they do not direct the individual to the present
as well as to the past and future. The player lives a sanctified
life. He does not alternately fight the world and escape from
it as the secular worker does, nor does he usefully and abu-
sively covenant with it as the magical worker does. Rather,
the full adult adventurer is in communion with the world,
demonstrating the love that is identical to that expressed by
the gods in their creation of the world in the beginning. The
paradise of the player is here and now. What happens to the
child in play can happen to the adult. And when it does,
paradise is present.

Irrelevance and Irreverence. Play is irrelevant to the
world and irreverent to God. Such praise of play is not likely
to be meaningful to those of the contemporary church who
desire to be relevant and reverent. Yet the religious individual always has been and will be irrelevant and irreverent.

There is much in current American leisure activities that
leads critics of culture to assume that play is superficial and
selfish. One of the most abused terms of our time is "fun."
Popular culture seems to consist almost entirely of fun with
toys, whether it be fun with cooking, fun with painting and
music, fun with mathematics and philosophy, fun with children, fun with sex, fun with war, or even fun with God.
This fun is easy and pleasurable, the motto behind it being,
"No strain and no pain." It is superficial because it avoids
the heights and depths of life by attenuating human responses. And it is selfish because it uses other people for the

sake of private pleasure. The funsters seek diversion from work, but the result is only diversion from life.

The spirit of play is not the same as the spirit of fun that is being promoted in our time. The funsters are actually workers who deny their inner state. Their fun occurs to facilitate either relaxation from past work or refreshment for future work. It is a retreat for the sake of escape from, or preparation for, work. The behavior of the funsters mocks play by aping it, and this is the last resort of those whose inner conflict is severe. So the player is totally different from the funster. For the former, play serves no purpose, not even that of distraction. It is unrelated to work in every way. The life of the funster is quite relevant to the world of work and reflects the desperation and despair of the worker. The life of the player is quite irrelevant to the work world and reflects all the characteristics of a new world. Play is irrelevant to the world of work.

The funster is superficial, whereas the player is serious. In commenting on the maturity of man, Nietzsche said, "that means to have reacquired the seriousness that one had as a child at play."[7] Those who have observed children at play have no doubt about their seriousness. One has only to be a spoilsport by interfering with their game, or, even worse, by breaking their rules, to discover how they take their play. Now the funster is not serious (at least, on the surface) and the worker is serious, yet the attitude of the player differs from both. De Quincey is reported to have said that a man is disguised by sobriety rather than by intoxication. The seriousness of the worker is sober and conceals his inner conflict. The seriousness of the player is drunken and reveals his inner harmony. So the adventures granted by the spirit of play are not sugar-coated. Rather, what distinguishes such activity from work is that it is not coated with bile. For the player, the world of work is irrelevant.

It has already been asserted that the funster is selfish, whereas the player is social. The funster and the more obvious worker are both selfish, despite their proclamations to the contrary. The needs of, and good deeds done for, his neighbors are perceived and acted upon for his own sake. But the player has no inner conflict and, therefore, no need to be concerned about himself. He is free to respond to other people for their sakes. He does not suffer for himself, but suffers for others. Only the player is capable of love. The suffering engendered by this love is so different from that experienced by the worker as to merit a different label. Again, for the player, the world of work is irrelevant.

The above comments should not be taken to reflect a utopian dismissal of work. For the player, work is nearly a necessary evil. Its merit is that it provides the setting in which the spirit of play can be made known. As has been repeatedly affirmed, the sacred and profane are antagonistic but yet complementary. "All play and no work makes no Jack." The player experiences more than the worker can even hope for in the here and now. It is the worker who seeks the ultimate diversion found in utopias. Such flight is not necessary for one who has already been found by the spirit of play. Play is irrelevant to the world, but it occurs in the world and renders work irrelevant.

Play is also irreverent to God. A call to full mature play has been given in those affirmations which proclaim that the chief end of man is to "Delight in the Lord'" and to "Glorify God and enjoy him forever." This call has been responded to negatively.

Several thousand years ago, King David was bringing the Ark of God into a city. This was a serious and awesome responsibility. Only a few months before a man had died at the hand of the Lord for absent-mindedly touching the Ark. Yet it is recorded that David played before the Lord. With much shouting and leaping, he displayed his melodious voice and grace of movement before the Holy. His wife, and probably most of those who observed him, knew him to be irreverent and so disapproved. But the Lord approved. She was made barren for the rest of her days and David was blessed. Two hundred years ago, when the church still sponsored the education of children, the following rule was created:

> We prohibit play in the strongest terms. . . . The students shall rise at five o'clock in the morning, summer and winter. . . . The student shall be indulged with nothing which the world calls play. Let this rule be observed with strictest nicety; for those who play when they are young will play when they are old.[8]

Unfortunately, the church and school were successful, and the children could not play when they grew into maturity. They could not permit themselves to be irreverent. And like David's wife, their lives were made barren by the Lord. Despite a clear call, man has refused to delight in and enjoy his God.

Many contemporary Christians appear to be taking the advice of the Apostle Paul to "work out your own salvation with fear and trembling" out of context. The context reveals that Paul is leaving his friends and simply advising them to remain humble and continue to serve God. He follows this famous phrase by clearly stating that it is God who is the author of salvation. The Christians who work out their salvation with fear and trembling before their fellow men are secular workers. The Christians who work out their salvation in this manner before their Lord are magicians. In either case they work for their own sake. The reward is hell, the hell that is eternal work. It is no wonder many believers have noted that they would be bored and unhappy in heaven. They are too well adjusted to the future eternity which is their likely lot. Who could be more reverent before God than the working Satan, and who could be less reverent than the playing cherubim? The reverent Christian reveals a peculiar attitude.

It should be observed that not all the church's frequent criticism of leisure-time activities has been entirely misbegotten. Its criticism has occasionally been unwittingly reasonable because leisure activities may be only profane work disguised as diversion, or magical use of playtime, or, at best, immature religion. However, the modern gamester or sportsman may reply that immature religion is better than no religion at all, and that the church seems to be comprised of profane social routines and magical rites. The goal for the church is to encourage play on all levels. The task of the average person is to continue his playing and allow the spirit of full play to enter into all levels of his adult life. Thus, the church may assist the culture and the culture assist the church in order that the idolatrous attachment to the work world be diminished and the playful response to God be enhanced. In other words, the goal is to have hell recognized as hell and heaven recognized as heaven.

Play is irrelevant to the world and irreverent to God. The spirit of play that removes the barrenness of our lives is contained in the words of a religious player, Coventry Patmore:

> If we may credit certain hints contained in the lives of the saints, love raises the spirit above the sphere of reverence and worship into one of laughter and dalliance; a sphere in which the soul says:
>
> > "Shall I, a gnat which dances in thy ray,
> > Dare to be reverent?"[9]

Yes, only an irreverent gnat, but what dance!

We have made no attempt to suggest a specifically Christian doctrine of play. That would be another adventure which is yet to come. Our essay has only been an essay in praise of play. But the author may well be as much a worker as anyone else. What could be more likely for a member of contemporary society? It is probable that the real player does not praise play in general, but lives in praise of the specific adventure in which he is a participant. Our destiny is to become tellers of sacred stories and players of sacred games, but it will always be a specific story and game that captures the individual. A description of the adventure is impossible until it occurs to surprise the player.

This is a destiny of which we are little aware. Modern man is like the tiger cub who was raised by goats to bleat and nibble grass.[10] One night, when the cub was nearing maturity, an old tiger attacked the goats. Seeing that caricature of the real thing, the old tiger demanded: "What are you doing here among these goats? What are you chewing there? Why do you make this silly sound?" Before an answer was possible, the tiger seized the cub, carried him to a clear pond, and forced him to look at the reflection. "Now look at those two faces. Are they not alike? You have the pot face of a tiger; it is like mine. Why do you fancy yourself to be a goat? Why do you bleat? Why do you nibble grass?" The old one continued his educational program by forcing the frightened cub to eat a bleeding piece of raw meat. The morsel was tough and caused difficulty, but just as he was about to make his little noise again, he experienced the taste of blood. A strange feeling traveled through his body, his lips smacked, his back arched, his tail lashed the ground, and then, from his throat came the awesome, exultant roar of a tiger. The old tiger, gruffly accepting the transformation, responded: "Come, we shall go now for a hunt together in the jungle."

Modern man's nibbling on intellectual fodder and bleating of "existential" complaints has led him far astray from his true destiny and rendered him a caricature of his true nature. What is required to start him on his pilgrimage is a taste of the sacred story and sacred game that are high adventure. This is not a plea for modern man to go forth and play fully. Play at any level cannot be forced. But every man can keep his eyes open for a taste of something other than his usual grass. And who knows what form the great cat will take which initiates play adventure? It may be a tiger, but it may be a lion or leopard instead. It is our destiny to participate in a Surprise.

Notes

Preface

[1] Robert Havighurst, "The Nature and Values of Meaningful Free-Time Activity," *Aging and Leisure,* Robert W. Kleemeier (ed.) (New York: Oxford University Press, 1961), p. 310.

[2] Harvey Cox, *The Secular City* (New York: The Macmillan Company, 1965), p. 187.

[3] Robert Lee, *Religion and Leisure in America* (Nashville: Abingdon Press, 1964), p. 34.

1. Play as Play

[1] Mark Twain, *The Adventures of Tom Sawyer* (New York: Grosset and Dunlap, Inc., 1946), pp. 15–18.

[2] J. C. Friedrich von Schiller, "Letters upon the Aesthetic Education of Man," *Literary and Philosophical Essays,* Vol. 32 of *The Harvard Classics,* ed. Charles W. Eliot (New York: P. F. Collier and Son Company, 1910), Letter XXVII, p. 310.

[3] *Ibid.,* p. 266.

[4] Sigmund Freud, *Delusion and Dream and Other Essays,* trans. Harry Zohn, I. F. Grant Duff, James Strachey, Douglas Bryan, and Helen M. Downey (Boston: The Beacon Press, 1956), pp. 123–25; *Beyond the Pleasure Principle,* trans. James Strachey (New York: Bantam Books, 1959), pp. 32–36.

[5] Erik H. Erikson, *Childhood and Society* (New York: W. W. Norton and Company, Inc., 1950), p. 185.

[6] *Ibid.,* p. 186.

[7] *Ibid.,* p. 195.

[8] Erikson, "Configurations in Play—Clinical Notes," *The Psychoanalytic Quarterly,* VI (April, 1937), pp. 185–214.

[9] Erikson, *Childhood and Society,* p. 185.

[10] *Ibid.,* p. 184.

[11] Sigmund Freud, *Civilization and Its Discontents,* trans. Joan Riviere (Garden City, N.Y.: Doubleday & Company, Inc., 1958), p. 105.

[12] S. Ferenczi, *Final Contributions to the Problems and Methods of Psychoanalysis,* ed. M. Balint, trans. E. Mosbacher and others (London: Hogarth Press and the Institute of Psychoanalysis, 1955), p. 246.

[13] Norman O. Brown, *Life Against Death: The Psychoanalytical Meaning of History* (New York: Vintage Books, Alfred A. Knopf, Inc., and Random House, Inc., 1961), p. 175.

[14] Norman O. Brown, *Love's Body* (New York: Random House, 1966), p. 226.

[15] Brown, *Life Against Death,* p. 33.

[16] *Ibid.,* p. 308.

[17] Herbert Spencer, *The Principles of Psychology* (New York: D. Appleton and Company, 1873), II, pp. 629 ff.

[18] G. T. W. Patrick, *The Psychology of Relaxation* (Boston and New York: Houghton Mifflin Company, 1916), pp. 48 ff.

[19] Karl Groos, *The Play of Animals,* trans. Elizabeth L. Baldwin (New York: D. Appleton & Company, 1898); *The Play of Man,* trans. Elizabeth L. Baldwin (New York: D. Appleton and Company, 1901).

[20] Groos, *The Play of Man,* p. 3.

[21] Twain, *op. cit.,* p. 19.

2.   Play as Adventure

[1] Groos, *The Play of Man,* pp. 384–85.

[2] *Ibid.,* p. 385.

[3] Johan Huizinga, *Homo Ludens: A Study of the Play Element in Culture* (Boston: The Beacon Press, 1955), pp. 13–14.

[4] *Ibid.,* p. 14.

[5] Groos, *The Play of Man,* pp. 387–88.

[6] *Ibid.,* p. 388.

[7] Roger Caillois, *Man, Play, and Games,* trans. Meyer Barash (New York: The Free Press of Glencoe, Inc., a Division of the Crowell-Collier Publishing Company, 1961), p. 19.

[8] Huizinga, *op. cit.,* p. 50.

[9] *Ibid.,* p. 13.

[10] Caillois, *op. cit.,* p. 8.

[11] *Ibid.,* p. 8.

[12] *Ibid.,* p. 73.

3. Possibilities of Play

[1] Caillois, *Man, Play and Games,* p. 49.

[2] *Ibid.,* pp. 46–49.

[3] Schiller, "Letters upon the Aesthetic Education of Man," in *op. cit.*

[4] Huizinga, *Homo Ludens: A Study of the Play Element in Culture,* p. 46.

[5] Caillois, *op. cit.*

[6] *Ibid.,* p. 64.

[7] Huizinga, *op. cit.,* p. 211.

[8] *Ibid.,* p. 14.

[9] Roger Caillois, "Play and the Sacred," *Man and the Sacred,* trans. Meyer Barash (Glencoe, Ill.: The Free Press, 1959), pp. 152–62.

[10] Caillois, "Play and the Sacred," p. 159.

[11] *Ibid.,* p. 157.

[12] *Ibid.,* p. 158.

[13] *Ibid.,* p. 160.

4. Play and Religion

[1] Henry Fielding, *Tom Jones* (New York: Random House, 1964), p. 84.

[2] Rudolf Otto, *The Idea of the Holy,* trans. John W. Harvey, second edition (London: Oxford University Press, 1950), p. 26.

[3] Gerardus Van der Leeuw, *Religion in Essence and Manifestation,* trans. J. E. Turner (New York: Harper & Row, 1963), p. 23.

[4] Mircea Eliade, *The Sacred and the Profane: The Nature of Religion,* trans. Willard R. Trask (New York: Harcourt, Brace and Company, 1959), p. 10.

[5] Mircea Eliade, *Patterns in Comparative Religion,* trans. Rosemary Sheed (New York: Sheed & Ward, Inc., 1958), p. 13.

[6] Caillois, *Man and the Sacred,* p. 19.

[7] *Ibid.,* p. 22.

[8] Otto, *op. cit.,* p. 24.

[9] Van der Leeuw, *op. cit.,* p. 47.

[10] R. H. Codrington, "Religion," *The Melanesians: Studies in Their Anthropology and Folklore,* Chap. 7 (Oxford: Clarendon Press, 1891), pp. 118–20.

[11] Van der Leeuw, *op. cit.,* p. 24.

[12] Otto, *op. cit.*, p. 31.

[13] Van der Leeuw, *op. cit.*, p. 465.

[14] Caillois, *Man and the Sacred*, p. 22.

[15] Eliade, *Patterns in Comparative Religion*, pp. 17–18.

[16] Caillois, *Man and the Sacred*, p. 36.

[17] Eliade, *The Sacred and the Profane*, p. 213.

[18] Otto, *op. cit.*, p. 121.

[19] Van der Leeuw, *op. cit.*, p. 468.

[20] *Ibid.*, p. 546.

[21] *Ibid.*, p. 547.

[22] *Ibid.*, p. 545.

[23] Goethe, *Faust*, Part II, Act 5.

[24] Bronislaw Malinowski, "Culture," *Encyclopaedia of the Social Sciences*, IV (New York: The Macmillan Company, 1931), pp. 638–39.

[25] Van der Leeuw, *op. cit.*, p. 470.

[26] Caillois, *Man and the Sacred*, pp. 163–80.

5. Play, Myth, and Ritual

[1] Clyde Kluckhohn, "Myths and Rituals: A General Theory," *The Harvard Theological Review*, XXXV (January, 1942), p. 45.

[2] Samuel Henry Hooke, ed., *Myth and Ritual: Essays on the Myth and Ritual of the Hebrews in Relation to the Culture Pattern of the Ancient East* (London: Oxford University Press, 1933), and *The Labyrinth: Further Studies in the Relation Between Myth and Ritual in the Ancient World* (New York: The Macmillan Company, 1935).

[3] Kluckhohn, *op. cit.*, pp. 59–64.

[4] Mircea Eliade, *Myth and Reality*, trans. Willard R. Trask, Vol. XXXI of *World Perspectives Series*, ed. Ruth Nanda Anshen (New York: Harper & Row, 1963), pp. 18–19.

[5] Eliade, *Patterns in Comparative Religion*, p. 397.

[6] Eliade, *Myth and Reality*, p. 54.

[7] Eliade, *Patterns in Comparative Religion*, p. 418.

[8] Eliade, *The Sacred and the Profane*, p. 96.

[9] Van der Leeuw, *op. cit.*, pp. 415 ff.

[10] Eliade, *Myth and Reality*, pp. 8–9.

[11] *Ibid.*, p. 11.

[12] Mircea Eliade, *Cosmos and History: The Myth of the Eternal Return*, trans. Willard R. Trask (New York: Harper & Row, 1959), pp. 85–86.

[13] James A. Teit, *Mythology of the Thompson Indians*, Publication

of the Jessup North Pacific Expedition, Vol. 8, Pt. 2 (Leiden and New York: Brill and Stechert, 1912), pp. 321–22.

[14] Gerardus Van der Leeuw, *Sacred and Profane Beauty: The Holy in Art,* trans. David E. Green (New York: Holt, Rinehart & Winston, 1963), p. 95.

[15] Sebastian de Grazia, *Of Time, Work and Leisure* (Garden City, N.Y.: Anchor Books, Doubleday & Company, Inc., 1962), p. 290.

[16] Robert R. Marett, *The Threshold of Religion,* second edition (New York: The Macmillan Company, 1914), p. 45.

[17] Huizinga, *Homo Ludens: A Study of the Play Element in Culture,* p. 139.

[18] William A. Lessa and Evon Z. Vogt, *Reader in Comparative Religion,* second edition (New York: Harper & Row, 1965), p. 142.

[19] Van der Leeuw, *Religion in Essence and Manifestation,* p. 340.

[20] Eliade, *The Sacred and the Profane,* p. 22.

[21] *Ibid.,* p. 21.

[22] *Ibid.,* p. 64.

[23] Van der Leeuw, *Sacred and Profane Beauty,* p. 37.

[24] *Ibid.,* p. 14.

[25] *Ibid.,* p. 17.

[26] *Ibid.,* p. 29.

[27] *Ibid.,* p. 30.

[28] Ruth M. Underhill, *Red Man's Religion: Beliefs and Practices of the Indians North of Mexico* (Chicago: The University of Chicago Press, 1965), p. 245.

[29] Huizinga, *op. cit.,* pp. 164–65.

[30] William F. Goode, *Religion Among the Primitives* (Glencoe, Ill.: The Free Press, 1951), p. 46.

[31] Royden Keith Yerkes, *Sacrifice in Greek and Roman Religions and Early Judaism* (New York: Charles Scribner's Sons, 1952), p. 5.

[32] Caillois, *Man and the Sacred,* p. 28.

[33] Van der Leeuw, *Religion in Essence and Manifestation,* p. 343.

[34] *Ibid.,* p. 351.

6.   In Praise of Play

[1] Robert Lee, *Religion and Leisure in America* (Nashville: Abingdon Press, 1964), p. 17.

[2] Franz Alexander, "A Contribution to the Theory of Play," *The Psychoanalytic Quarterly,* XXVII (April, 1958), p. 192.

[3] Heinrich Zimmer, as quoted by Mircea Eliade, *Myths, Dreams, and Mysteries* (New York: Harper & Row, 1960), p. 245.

[4] Geoffrey Gorer, *Death, Grief, and Mourning* (New York: Doubleday & Company, Inc., 1965), pp. 192–201.

[5] Mircea Eliade, *Birth and Rebirth: The Religious Meanings of Initiation in Human Culture,* trans. Willard R. Trask (New York: Harper & Row, 1958), p. xiii; *The Sacred and the Profane,* p. 201.

[6] Eliade, *Patterns in Comparative Religion,* p. 408.

[7] Friedrich Nietzsche, "Beyond Good and Evil," trans. Helen Zimmern, *The Philosophy of Nietzsche* (New York: The Modern Library, 1927), p. 456.

[8] Harry Emerson Fosdick, "Living for the Fun of it," *American Magazine* (April, 1930), cited by Karl Menninger with the collaboration of Jeanette Lyle Menninger, *Love Against Hate* (New York: Harcourt, Brace and Company, 1942), p. 167.

[9] Coventry Patmore, *The Rod, the Root, and the Flower,* "Aurea Dicta," 39 (London: 1907).

[10] Heinrich Zimmer, *Philosophies of India,* ed. Joseph Campbell (New York: Pantheon Books, Inc., 1951), pp. 5–8.

Bibliography

Alexander, Franz. "A Contribution to the Theory of Play," *The Psychoanalytic Quarterly*, XXVII (April, 1958), pp. 175–93.

Brown, Norman O. *Life Against Death: The Psychoanalytical Meaning of History*. New York: Vintage Books, Alfred A. Knopf, Inc., and Random House, Inc., 1961.

———. *Love's Body*. New York: Random House, 1966.

Caillois, Roger. *Man, Play, and Games*. Trans. Meyer Barash. New York: The Free Press of Glencoe, Inc., A Division of the Crowell-Collier Publishing Company, 1961.

———. "Play and the Sacred," *Man and the Sacred*. Trans. Meyer Barash. Glencoe, Ill.: The Free Press, a Corporation, 1959.

Codrington, R. H. "Religion," *The Melanesians: Studies in Their Anthropology and Folklore*. Oxford: Clarendon Press, 1891.

Cox, Harvey. *The Secular City*. New York: The Macmillan Company, 1965.

Eliade, Mircea. *Birth and Rebirth: The Religious Meanings of Initiation in Human Culture*. Trans. Willard R. Trask. New York: Harper & Row, 1958.

———. *Cosmos and History: The Myth of the Eternal Return*. Trans. Willard R. Trask. New York: Harper Torchbooks, Harper & Row, 1959.

———. *Myth and Reality*. Trans. Willard R. Trask. Vol. XXXI of *World Perspectives Series*. Edited by Ruth Nanda Anshen. New York: Harper & Row, 1963.

———. *Myths, Dreams and Mysteries: The Encounter between Contemporary Faiths and Archaic Realities*. Trans. Philip Mairet. In *The Library of Religion and Culture*. Edited by Benjamin Nelson. New York: Harper & Row, 1960.

———. *Patterns in Comparative Religion: A Study of the Element of the Sacred in the History of Religious Phenomena*. Trans. Rosemary Sheed. New York: Sheed & Ward, Inc., 1958.

———. *The Sacred and the Profane: The Nature of Religion.* Trans. Willard R. Trask. New York: Harcourt, Brace and Company, 1959.

Erikson, Erik H. *Childhood and Society.* New York: W. W. Norton & Company, Inc., 1950.

———. "Configurations in Play—Clinical Notes," *The Psychoanalytic Quarterly,* VI (April, 1937), pp. 139–214.

Ferenczi, S. *Final Contributions to the Problems and Methods of Psychoanalysis.* Trans. E. Mosbacher and others. Edited by M. Balint. London: Hogarth Press and the Institute of Psychoanalysis, 1955.

Fielding, Henry. *Tom Jones.* New York: Random House, 1964.

Freud, Sigmund. *Beyond the Pleasure Principle.* Trans. James Strachey. New York: Bantam Books, 1959.

———. *Civilization and Its Discontents.* Trans. Joan Riviere. Garden City, N.Y.: Doubleday & Company, Inc., 1958.

———. *Delusion and Dream and Other Essays.* Trans. Harry Zohn, I. F. Grant Duff, James Strachey, Douglas Bryan, and Helen M. Downey. Boston: The Beacon Press, 1956.

Goode, William F. *Religion Among the Primitives.* Glencoe, Ill.: The Free Press, a Corporation, 1951.

Gorer, Geoffrey. *Death, Grief, and Mourning.* New York: Doubleday & Company, Inc., 1965.

Grazia, Sebastian de. *Of Time, Work and Leisure.* New York: Doubleday & Company, Inc., 1962.

Groos, Karl. *The Play of Animals.* Trans. Elizabeth L. Baldwin. New York: D. Appleton & Company, 1898.

———. *The Play of Man.* Trans. Elizabeth L. Baldwin. New York: D. Appleton & Company, 1901.

Havighurst, Robert. "The Nature and Values of Meaningful Free-Time Activity," *Aging and Leisure.* Edited by Robert W. Kleemeier. New York: Oxford University Press, 1961.

Hooke, Samuel Henry (ed.). *The Labyrinth: Further Studies in the Relation Between Myth and Ritual in the Ancient World.* New York: The Macmillan Company, 1935.

———. *Myth and Ritual: Essays on the Myth and Ritual of the Hebrews in Relation to the Culture Pattern of the Ancient East.* London: Oxford University Press, 1933.

Huizinga, Johan. *Homo Ludens: A Study of the Play Element in Culture.* Boston: The Beacon Press, 1955.

Kluckhohn, Clyde. "Myths and Rituals: A General Theory," *The Harvard Theological Review,* XXXV (January, 1942), p. 45.

Lee, Robert. *Religion and Leisure in America*. Nashville: Abingdon Press, 1964.

Lessa, William A., and Evon Z. Vogt. *Reader in Comparative Religion*, Second Edition. New York: Harper & Row, 1965.

Malinowski, Bronislaw. "Culture," *Encyclopaedia of the Social Sciences*, IV. New York: The Macmillan Company, 1931.

Marett, Robert R. *The Threshold of Religion*. Second Edition. New York: The Macmillan Company, 1914.

Menninger, Karl, and Jeanette Lyle Menninger. *Love Against Hate*. New York: A Harvest Book, Harcourt, Brace and Company, 1942.

Nietzsche, Friedrich. "Beyond Good and Evil," *The Philosophy of Nietzsche*. Trans. Helen Zimmern. New York: The Modern Library, 1927.

Otto, Rudolf. *The Idea of the Holy*. Trans. John W. Harvey. Second Edition. London: Oxford University Press, 1950.

Patmore, Coventry. *The Rod, the Root, and the Flower*, "Aurea Dicta," 39. London: 1907.

Patrick, G. T. W. *The Psychology of Relaxation*. Boston and New York: Houghton Mifflin Company, 1916.

Spencer, Herbert. *The Principles of Psychology*. New York: D. Appleton and Company, 1873.

Teit, James A. *Mythology of the Thompson Indians* (Publication of the Jessup North Pacific Expedition, Vol. 8, Pt. 2). Leiden and New York: Brill and Slechert, 1912.

Twain, Mark. *The Adventures of Tom Sawyer*. New York: Grosset & Dunlap Inc., 1946.

Underhill, Ruth M. *Red Man's Religion: Beliefs and Practices of the Indians North of Mexico*. Chicago: The University of Chicago Press, 1965.

Van der Leeuw, Gerardus. *Religion in Essence and Manifestation*. Trans. J. E. Turner. New York: Harper & Row, 1963.

———. *Sacred and Profane Beauty: The Holy in Art*. Trans. David E. Green. New York: Holt, Rinehart & Winston, 1963.

von Schiller, J. C. Friedrich. "Letters upon the Aesthetic Education of Man," *Literary and Philosophical Essays*, Vol. 32 of *The Harvard Classics*, Charles W. Eliot, editor. New York: P. F. Collier & Son Company, 1910. Pp. 221–313.

Yerkes, Royden Keith. *Sacrifice in Greek and Roman Religions and Early Judaism*. New York: Charles Scribner's Sons, 1952.

Zimmer, Heinrich. *Philosophies of India*. Edited by Joseph Campbell. New York: Pantheon Books, Inc., 1951.

Designed by Ellen Brecher
Set in Caledonia
Composed and printed by York Composition Company, Inc.
Bound by The Haddon Craftsmen, Inc.
HARPER & ROW, PUBLISHERS, INCORPORATED

69 70 71 72 73 8 7 6 5 4 3 2 1